Learning Through Play in the Primary School

Drawing on research to inform practice, this book is written for teachers and school leaders looking for guidance on how to successfully implement a play-based curriculum in the early years of primary school.

Learning Through Play in the Primary School unpacks the "why" and the "how" of embedding play-based pedagogies in the first three years of school. The book is divided into two sections, the first drawing on the latest research to outline the importance of play in a child's development and emotional engagement in learning. The second section provides practical support and examples for how to embed play in a school curriculum to enhance young children's learning. The practical section covers setting up an environment for guided play, demonstrating how to assess learning from play-based activities and how to report on outcomes, supported by checklists, vignettes, and case studies.

Written to facilitate the implementation of play-based learning in the primary school years, this book will be an essential guide for pre- and in-service teachers and school leaders.

Louise Paatsch, Ph.D., is Professor in the School of Education at Deakin University, Australia. Her areas of research include children's language, pretend play, and digital play, with a strong focus on metapragmatic and pragmatic language use. She also explores teachers' talk patterns in supporting children's language and play abilities.

Siobhan Casey, Ph.D., is a paediatric occupational therapist with extensive experience in working with children, families, and educators. She is a Supervisor with the Masters of Child Play Therapy, Deakin University, and delivers training, both nationally and internationally, through Learn To Play, Melbourne. She has a strong passion for supporting play-based learning in schools.

Amity Green, MAChPT, BASocWk, PGDipL&T, is an Academic and Supervisor in the Master of Child Play Therapy course, Deakin University, Australia. She is a registered Social Worker, Play Therapist and a registered teacher with Education Queensland, working with families and teachers of children requiring additional support at home and in mainstream schooling.

Karen Stagnitti, Ph.D., is Emeritus Professor in the School of Health and Social Development, Deakin University, Geelong, Australia. She has researched play for over three decades, working with families, teachers, community services, and schools. She has developed four play assessments and a therapeutic play approach called Learn to Play Therapy.

Learning Through Play in the Primary School

The Why and the How for Teachers and School Leaders

Louise Paatsch, Siobhan Casey, Amity Green and Karen Stagnitti

Routledge
Taylor & Francis Group

LONDON AND NEW YORK

Designed cover image: © Getty Images

First published 2024
by Routledge
4 Park Square, Milton Park, Abingdon, Oxon OX14 4RN

and by Routledge
605 Third Avenue, New York, NY 10158

Routledge is an imprint of the Taylor & Francis Group, an informa business

© 2024 Louise Paatsch, Siobhan Casey, Amity Green, and Karen Stagnitti

The right of Louise Paatsch, Siobhan Casey, Amity Green, and Karen Stagnitti to be identified as authors of this work has been asserted in accordance with sections 77 and 78 of the Copyright, Designs and Patents Act 1988.

British Library Cataloguing-in-Publication Data
A catalogue record for this book is available from the British Library

Library of Congress Cataloging-in-Publication Data
Names: Paatsch, Louise, author. | Casey, Siobhan, author. | Green, Amity, author. | Stagnitti, Karen, author.
Title: Learning through play in the primary school : the why and the how for teachers and school leaders / Louise Paatsch, Siobhan Casey, Amity Green, Karen Stagnitti.
Description: Abingdon, Oxon ; New York : Routledge, 2024. | Includes bibliographical references and index.
Identifiers: LCCN 2023013678 (print) | LCCN 2023013679 (ebook) | ISBN 9781032284231 (hardback) | ISBN 9781032284217 (paperback) | ISBN 9781003296782 (ebook)
Subjects: LCSH: Play. | Education, Primary. | Child development.
Classification: LCC LB1137 .P22 2024 (print) | LCC LB1137 (ebook) | DDC 155.4/18--dc23/eng/20230605
LC record available at https://lccn.loc.gov/2023013678
LC ebook record available at https://lccn.loc.gov/2023013679

ISBN: 978-1-032-28423-1 (hbk)
ISBN: 978-1-032-28421-7 (pbk)
ISBN: 978-1-003-29678-2 (ebk)

DOI: 10.4324/9781003296782

Typeset in Galliard
by Taylor & Francis Books

Contents

Illustrations

Figures

Tables

Boxes

Acknowledgments

We would like to acknowledge all the children, teachers, and principals we have worked with over the years. Thank you for sharing your knowledge, opinions, and practices with us. We appreciate with gratitude the privilege of observing the play of all the children we have worked with over that time. We have learnt so much from you all.

Section 1

The Why

1   Why Play in Schools?

What is play?

Defining play has been an area of great interest and debate amongst researchers, philosophers, teachers, and parents for many years. However, despite the challenge in establishing one universal definition, it is well known that play is complex, is at the very heart of childhood, and is an essential part of children's learning and development (Clements & Fiorentino, 2004; Grieshaber & Barnes, 2021; Yogman et al., 2018; Zosh et al., 2018). Vygotsky (1967) theorised that through play, children learn, particularly when they play with a more competent other (e.g., parent or more competent peer). This socio-cultural development theory highlights the importance of social interactions and the influence of the child's social and cultural environments on their learning and development (Vygotsky, 1967).

Play includes many activities, from physical rough and tumble play, to block and game play, to pretend or imaginative play. Many researchers have often described play according to its specific features and characteristics. For example, Gray (2009) suggests five key characteristics of play, including: "(1) self-chosen and self-directed; (2) intrinsically motivated; (3) structured by mental rules; (4) imaginative; and (5) produced in an active, alert, but non-stressed frame of mind" (p. 480). Similarly, other researchers posit that common characteristics of play include flexibility (e.g., use of objects in new combinations, different roles), nonliterality (e.g., behaviours that lack their usual meaning), positive affect (e.g., laughter, enjoyment, fun), and pretense (e.g., pretending with actions and objects) (Lillard et al., 2013; Smith, 2005). In a more recent study, Zosh et al. (2018) explored the literature on play and learning and suggested that children experience joy and have agency in play, and that play may take on various forms. They suggest a multi-dimensional definition of play where play is positioned as meaningful, joyful, and iterative where children are engaged and active. Play is also described as being voluntary, spontaneous, fun, and often without extrinsic goals – an activity where the process is more important than the end point or goal (Smith, 2005; Yogman et al. 2018).

Many researchers also describe play according to the different types, including functional play (e.g., using objects as their intended purpose), construction play

DOI: 10.4324/9781003296782-2

(e.g., building a tower from blocks), pretend play (also known as symbolic, dramatic or imaginative play – the child's use of symbols in their play), games with rules (e.g., chasing or digital games), auditory play (e.g., listening to music and acting out), physical or gross motor play (e.g., climbing on play equipment), sensorimotor play (e.g., playing with objects in a sand pit or in a water tray), language play (e.g., playing with sounds, noises, and words), and visual perceptual play (e.g., jigsaw puzzles) (Lillard et al., 2013; Robertson et al., 2020). Zosh et al. (2018) suggest that play should be viewed as a spectrum that ranges from free play to direct instruction, in order to demonstrate the integration and complementary nature of different types of play. Specifically, they argue that in free play a child initiates and directs the play without adult guidance or scaffolding. However, in situations where a child directs the play within a context that has been set up by an adult around a learning goal, then it is guided play. During guided play, a child has agency around the ways in which the activities take shape. In contexts where the adult intervenes to direct the child's play, the play is no longer guided but co-opted. For example, a child may be setting up the scene of a farm and pretends that the farmer is milking the cows when the adult picks up the sheep and tells the child that the sheep needs some food. Such intervening by the adult redirects the play and may reduce the child's level of agency in directing the play. The final type of play on the spectrum is direct instruction where the play is initiated and directed by the adult with an explicit learning goal. We argue that this spectrum of play is heavily dependent on the different roles that the adult plays in scaffolding children's learning within the play and is not linear but rather interconnected (see Chapter 9 for further discussion around this spectrum of play). We also suggest that pretend play overlaps with other types of play. For example, when a child is pretending to be a superhero in their play, they may take on more physical play, or when the construction play with blocks becomes part of the scene within their play then this overlaps with pretend play.

In this book we focus on pretend play and its value in supporting children's learning and development. We also focus on the importance of guided play and the role of the teacher in scaffolding children to their next level of development.

What is pretend play?

Pretend play is "the non-literal use of objects, action or attributes … that appears to develop on a relatively fixed schedule and is present in every culture" (Creaghe et al., 2021, p. 981). Pretend play involves children's use of cognition and emotions as they use symbols to create stories in their play and imbue objects with imaginary functions and characteristics (Creaghe, 2020; Stagnitti, 2021). For example, a child may use a toy cup to drink a cup of tea when playing in the scene of a café, demonstrating their ability to use the object for its intended purpose. They may also begin to use the same object beyond its purpose by pretending the cup is a sunhat for a doll.

Many researchers have identified many distinctive behaviours in pretend play, including: (1) substituting objects; (2) role play within an imaginary context where a child can eventually maintain a role until the play is finished; (3) developing play scripts that include fictional stories with problems and resolutions that persist over time; (4) character play using dolls, figurines, teddies, etc., that may include the character that has separate life from the child; and (5) sequences of play actions which are organised, planned, logical, and become more complex over time (Elkonin, 2005; Robertson et al., 2020; Stagnitti & Paatsch, 2018).

According to cognitive and socio-cognitive theorists, pretend play is also social as children engage with others in the play. Vygotsky (1967) suggests that pretend play is the source of, and creates, a zone of proximal development (ZPD) for children's cognitive and language processes, including opportunities for rich dialogue and social use of language. This ZPD is the difference between the child's current level of independent performance and the level where the child can learn supported by capable adults and peers. Vygotsky proposed that

> In play a child is always above his average age, above his daily behavior; in play it is as though he were a head taller than himself. As in the focus of a magnifying glass, play contains all developmental tendencies in a condensed form; in play it is as though the child were trying to jump above the level of his normal behavior.
>
> (Vygotsky, 1967, p. 16)

Vygotsky's theory of play as creating the ZPD for children has been applied and expanded by other scholars and researchers over many years. Together, they "share the emphasis on play not as a reflection of past experiences but as an activity essential for the development of a 'future child'" (Bodrova & Leong, 2015, p. 377).

Rakoczy (2008) also suggests that play is social in origin and establishes shared intentionality. For example, in the early years of life children are highly supported and scaffolded by their parents and therefore pretence acts are "acquired through imitation in similar ways to other forms of action" (p. 506). Such environments also "cultivates children's understanding of the symbolic nature of the world the mind states of others" (Creaghe & Kidd, 2022, p. 1139). For example, let's consider Albert, a child in your classroom who is playing with their friend Enya in the café. Albert is in the role of customer and orders their meal from the menu. He has finished eating his sandwich then picks up a block and pretends that it is phone and taps it on the machine to pay for their food. Enya, in her role as the café owner, looks at Albert then smiles and says "thank you, I hope you enjoyed your sandwich". In this scenario Albert is demonstrating his ability to substitute and impose meaning on an object. In addition, there is implicit shared understanding between both children as they engage in joint attention and understanding of the intentionality of the action (i.e., the tapping of the block as a phone to pay). In this joint action there is, as Creaghe et al. (2021) describe, a "meeting of the minds" in that the transformation is successful when both children have the same "mental representation" (p. 982). Furthermore, both children also demonstrate an understanding of the rules of the play and the social norms of the cultural context (i.e., the payment for food and the thanking by the owner to the customer). As such, pretend play is an important context for children to learn and develop – a ZPD that provides a context to engage in the highest level of play as they interact with competent others to achieve the next step in their development (Creaghe et al., 2021; Quinn & Kidd, 2019; Stagnitti, 2021; Vygotsky, 1967).

What is the value of play?

> Play has value for the development of well-adjusted, creative individuals who will be prepared to solve challenging problems.
>
> (Weisburg et al., 2015, p. 12)

As researchers, educators, and therapists, we are often asked by school staff to provide reasons for why play should be embedded into the school curriculum. Questions posed often include "What is the value of play and how does it support children's learning? How does play link to other parts of the school curriculum?" In answering these questions, we initially draw on the evidence in the research and provide teachers with appropriate readings. We also support teachers to reflect on their own learnings after embedding play into their classrooms and answer these questions for themselves. For example, recently a government primary school in the western suburbs of Melbourne, Australia, embedded play into the curriculum. At the end of the year, the researchers (Nolan, Paatsch & Stagnitti – project called "Thinking differently about practice: Developmental Play") invited the teachers to reflect on the value of play for children in their classroom. From the 61 teacher responses, 11 main themes were identified including providing opportunities for children to: co-operate and co-construct; socialise; problem-solve; have fun and engage in the learning; support academic learning; support oral language; develop self-esteem; build independence; be scaffolded by others; and to support creativity. Such responses also reflect the large body of literature that has highlighted the importance of pretend play for children's cognitive, social, emotional, physical, and academic learning and development.

It is well established in the literature that play provides enormous value for children's learning and development. For example, Yogman et al. (2018) argued that play is fundamentally important for learning 21st Century skills, such as creativity, group work and collaboration, and problem solving. Such skills are critical skills for success in later life and are highlighted as important for teachers to develop in children in the Australian Curriculum within the General Capabilities.

Pretend play involves multiple areas of the brain, including areas that are responsible for higher-order thinking, creativity and imagination, self-awareness, emotion, pleasure, and motor control. Such experiences, which also include positive and responsive interactions with peers and adults, support children's brain development. In Chapter 2 of this book, we present a brief overview of the brain and some of the research evidence that shows the importance of play in supporting brain development. We also discuss the ways in which creating a sense of safety through play prepares children to be ready for learning. As children engage in play their decreased levels of stress and anxiety are evident, as well as increased levels of happiness, joy, and social awareness. Chapter 2 provides examples of the areas of the brain that are activated and integrated as children engage in pretend play. We also highlight the critical roles teachers play in providing rich and authentic experiences to support children's brain development and to promote a sense of safety for children to learn, to self-regulate, and experience the joy of learning.

There is a large body of research that shows the link between pretend play, language acquisition, and later literacy development including the development of children's syntactic, semantic, phonological awareness, pragmatic (social use of language), and narrative abilities. In Chapters 2 and 3, we outline the ways in which pretend play provides a fertile environment for children to develop narrative. For example, as children create stories in their play, they are able to introduce characters, plots, scenes, problems and resolutions. In Chapter 3 we also link narrative development to pragmatic language abilities where children take turns, self-regulate by taking the perspective of another person (i.e., Theory of Mind; also see Chapters 4 and 5) and can attribute mental states to themselves and others in the play (e.g., I think, he feels, etc.). We also provide practical examples to demonstrate the ways in which pretend play provides a social context in which children can develop pragmatic skills such as initiation, collaboration and negotiation, contingency, and conversational competence – abilities that lead to building friendships and social and emotional wellbeing.

Pretend play involves children's ability to understand and use emotion – a process that develops through interactions with others and also leads to the development of understanding character in story. Such interactions are important in fostering children's awareness of the world around them and their ability to self-regulate. In Chapter 4 we outline self-regulation, emotional understanding, and the strong link to pretend play. In particular, we present seven key components that make up the capacity of self-regulation, including intensity, sensitivity, specificity, windows of tolerance, recovery processes, access to consciousness, and external expression. Practical examples are also provided in this chapter to demonstrate the link between play, particularly guided play, and the important role of the teacher in supporting these abilities.

Given the strong link between pragmatic language abilities and children's abilities to use language in social contexts, it is not surprising that pretend play provides an authentic context for children to develop social capabilities. Research has also shown that there is a link between pretend play and social capabilities, including increased levels of collaboration and talk, and metacognitive behaviours (McAloney & Stagnitti, 2009; Whitebread & O'Sullivan, 2012; Yogman et al., 2018). For example, children who are able to create elaborate play scenes in their stories and substitute objects in their pretend play are often the same children whom their teachers report as being socially competent (McAloney & Stagnitti, 2009). In Chapter 5 of this book, we provide further discussion around the link between pretend play and the development of children's social capabilities. We also provide examples from teacher practice to demonstrate some of the ways to foster an environment that supports children's understanding of character, object substitution, and promotion of meaningful interactions with peers and others.

There is a strong link between pretend play, creativity, and storytelling. For example, to be creative in storytelling, children need to be able to create characters, scenes, and problems but also demonstrate flexible and divergent thinking. Play also provides children the freedom to explore, experiment, create, hypothesise, question, and experience a sense of agency. Chapter 6 provides a discussion of the research that has explored the relations between creativity, storytelling, and pretend play. It also describes some practical examples of these links in the classroom context, including the presentation of a play and storytelling program in a school in Victoria, Australia.

Pretend play also provides a rich context for supporting children's academic abilities, including English (i.e., language, literacy, and literature), mathematics, science, health and physical education, and the arts. In Chapter 7, we present examples from research that support this link between pretend play and these academic abilities. We also argue that play is not an add-on but rather a way of doing. As such, observing and supporting children's pretend play abilities also provide opportunities for teachers to observe and assess many of the learning areas outlined in government policies, frameworks, and curriculum guidelines including the Australian Curriculum and the Victorian Early Years Learning Framework.

Together, we argue that pretend play is a melting pot of ability. As represented in Figure 1.1, pretend play provides the context for children to develop many abilities, including metacommunication, verbal and non-verbal communication and language, narrative, metacommunication, creativity, creative and critical thinking, divergent thinking, and problem-solving. Pretend play also fosters children's self-regulation, self-awareness, and social skills. Pretend play is joyful, meaningful, iterative, socially interactive, flexible, and enables children to be agentic, active, and engaged in their own learning.

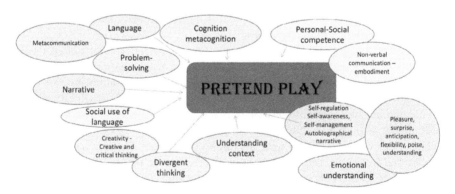

Figure 1.1 Pretend play: A melting pot of abilities

Conclusion

Embedding play into classrooms within the school context is critical. As high-lighted in this chapter and throughout other chapters in this book, pretend play is thinking play and provides a rich and authentic context for supporting children's cognitive, academic, physical, social, and emotional abilities.

The aim of this book is to support teachers to understand the value of play in children's lives and that play is a way of doing rather than an add-on. The book is divided into two sections. Section 1 (Chapters 1–6) provides research-based and practice-based evidence to advocate for the importance of play and the rationale for valuing play in schools. However, teachers often ask – "How do I set up pretend play in the classroom? What resources do I need? What is my role in the children's play? How do I assess and report children's play abilities? Can you provide me with some practical examples to support my understandings of play and the ways in which I can implement play into my classroom?" Section 2 (Chapters 7–11) provides some answers to these very complex questions. In particular, we provide research-based and practice-based evidence to support teachers' understandings and to advocate for the importance of embedding play in the curriculum.

References

Bodrova, E., & Leong, D. J. (2015). Vygotskian and post-Vygotskian views on children's play. *American Journal of Play*, 7(3), 371–388.

Clements, R. L., & Fiorentino, L. (Eds.) (2004). *The child's right to play: A global approach*. Greenwood Publishing Group.

Creaghe, N. V. (2020). Symbolic play and language acquisition: The dynamics of infant–caretaker communication during symbolic play. Unpublished doctoral dissertation, The Australian National University, Australia.

Creaghe, N., & Kidd, E. (2022). Symbolic play as a zone of proximal development: An analysis of informational exchange. *Social Development*, 31(4), 1138–1156. doi:10.1111.sode.12592.

Creaghe, N., Quinn, S., & Kidd, E. (2021). Symbolic play provides a fertile context for language development. *Infancy*, 26(6), 980–1010. doi:10.1111.infa.12422.

Edwards, S. (2021). Digital play and technical code: What new knowledge formations are possible?. *Learning, Media and Technology*, 46(3), 306–319.

Elkonin, D. B. (2005). The psychology of play. *Journal of Russian & East European Psychology*, 43(1), 11–21.

Gray, P. (2009). Play as a foundation for hunter-gatherer social existence. *American Journal of Play*, 1(4), 476–522.

Grieshaber, S., & Barnes, S. (2021). Playing with the politics of play. In T. Kinard & G. S. Cannella (Eds.), *Childhoods in more just worlds: An international handbook* (pp. 259–277). Myers Education Press.

Lillard, A. S., Lerner, M. D., Hopkins, E. J., Dore, R. A., Smith, E. D., & Palmquist, C. M. (2013). The impact of pretend play on children's development: A review of the evidence. *Psychological Bulletin*, 139(1), 1–34. doi:10.1037/a0029321.

Nolan, A., & Paatsch, L. (2018). (Re) affirming identities: Implementing a play-based approach to learning in the early years of schooling. *International Journal of Early Years Education*, 26(1), 42–55. doi:10.1080/09669760.2017.1369397.

McAloney, K., & Stagnitti, K. (2009). Pretend play and social play: The concurrent validity of the Child-Initiated Pretend Play Assessment. *International Journal of Play Therapy*, 18(2), 99–113. doi:10.1037/a0014559.

Quinn, S., & Kidd, E. (2019). Symbolic play promotes non-verbal communicative exchange in infant–caregiver dyads. *British Journal of Developmental Psychology*, 37(1), 33–50. doi:10.1111/bjdp.12251.

Rakoczy, H. (2008). Pretence as individual and collective intentionality. *Mind & Language*, 23(5), 499–517. doi:10.1111/j.1468–0017.2008.00357.x.

Robertson, N., Morrissey, A. M., & Moore, D. (2020). From boats to bushes: Environmental elements supportive of children's sociodramatic play outdoors. *Children's Geographies*, 18(2), 234–246. doi:10.1080/14733285.2019.1630714.

Smith, P. K. (2005). Play: Types and functions in human development. In B. J. Ellis & D. F. Bjorklund (Eds.), *Origins of the social mind: Evolutionary psychology and child development* (pp. 271–291). Guilford Press.

Stagnitti, K. (2021). Learn to play therapy: Principles, process and practical activities. Learn to Play. https://www.learntoplayevents.com/product/learn-to-play-therapy-principles-process-and-practical-activities/.

Vygotsky, L. S. (1967). Play and its role in the mental development of the child. *Soviet Psychology*, 5(3), 6–18.

Weisberg, D. S., Kittredge, A. K., Hirsh-Pasek, K., Golinkoff, R. M., & Klahr, D. (2015). Making play work for education. *Phi Delta Kappan*, 96(8), 8–13. doi:10.1177/0031721715583955.

Whitebread, D., & O'Sullivan, L. (2012). Preschool children's social pretend play: Supporting the development of metacommunication, metacognition and self-regulation. *International Journal of Play*, 1, 197–213. doi:10.1080/21594937.2012.693384.

Yogman, M., Garner, A., Hutchinson, J., Hirsh-Pasek, K., & Golinkoff, R. M. (2018). The power of play: A pediatric role in enhancing development in young children. *Pediatrics*, 142(3). doi:10.1542/peds.2018–2058.

Zosh, J. M., Hirsh-Pasek, K., Hopkins, E. J., Jensen, H., Liu, C., Neale, D., & Whitebread, D. (2018). Accessing the inaccessible: Redefining play as a spectrum. *Frontiers in Psychology*, 9, 1124. doi:10.3389/fpsyg.2018.01124.

2   The Brain, Learning, and Play

We now know that the brain is experience dependent (Panksepp & Biven, 2012; Siegel, 2012; Sunderland, 2007). This means that a child's experience does impact their developing brain. Newborn babies have approximately 200 billion brain cells; however, they have very few connections between those brain cells, particularly in areas of the brain that think, plan, reflect, and understand social and emotional cues (Sunderland, 2007). Positive and responsive interactions with adults and peers result in more connections within and across the structure of a child's brain (Sunderland, 2007). This makes the school experience and the child's relationship with their teacher very important, as children spend approximately just under 200 days at school during a school year. This chapter explores: (1) the importance of a safe school environment for a child's brain and learning, and (2) the areas of brain function activation that occur with the experience of play in the classroom. The chapter concludes with an explanation of how narrative integrates the brain.

A brief overview of the brain

Our brain carries within it a history of humankind (Sunderland, 2007). The oldest area of our brain has been referred to as the 'Reptilian Brain' (Sunderland, 2007, pp. 18–19). This part of our brain is deep within our brain structure and includes the brain stem and cerebellum (Nunn et al., 2008). It operates below our level of consciousness and is related to survival. It controls essential body functions for sustaining life, such as breathing, circulation, body temperature, hunger, eye blinking, and balance (Sunderland, 2007, p. 19). The next oldest area of the brain is the Mammalian Brain, also called the Emotional Brain or Limbic System. It is associated with the expression of strong emotions, memory, reward, social bonding, playfulness, and the urge to explore (Panksepp & Biven, 2012; Sunderland, 2007). It also operates subconsciously, below the level of our awareness. Sometimes this area is referred to as the subcortex and includes brain structures such as the amygdala, hippocampus, hypothalamus, and corpus callosum (Nunn et al., 2008). The third 'area' of the brain is the most recently evolved area, which envelopes the Reptilian and Mammalian Brain areas (Sunderland, 2007). It has been referred to as the Rational Brain or the Cerebral Cortex (Sunderland, 2007), and includes the frontal lobes or neocortex. This area of the brain includes

DOI: 10.4324/9781003296782-3

functions related to creativity and imagination, planning, thinking, problem solving, reasoning, self-awareness, kindness, and empathy (Sunderland, 2007). Brain
functions can also be conceptualised from front to back (for example, the front has
the frontal lobes, and the back has the cerebellum) and right and left sides of the
brain. The right side of the brain (or right hemisphere) processes non-verbal
information, conceives the whole, and is intuitive (Siegel, 2012). The left side of
the brain is analytical, puts ideas into language, and is logical (Siegel, 2012).

Because the developing brain of a child is experience dependent, responsive
teaching (that is responding to children with the belief that they are capable
beings) can have a positive impact on a child's Rational Brain. Responsive, positive
interaction increases connections, pathways, and brain chemical systems between
lower and higher areas of the brain so a child can control their emotions, process
thoughts calmly, and think through to a solution (Siegel, 2012; Sunderland,
2007). When the Rational Brain is cut off (or has limited connections) from the
social emotional systems in the Mammalian Brain, children are capable of being
very cruel to others (Sunderland, 2007). Building connections within regions of
the brain, then, is critical for a child's developing brain, for learning, and for the
development of social emotional intelligence, prosocial behaviours, positive peer
relationships, and teacher–student relationships.

Feeling safe means I'm ready to learn

Before children can learn or play, they need to feel safe. The feeling of safety and
of being safe are deep within our sense of being (Allison & Rossouw, 2013). The
Reptilian and Mammalian Brain areas register danger or a lack of safety before we
consciously recognise it or can put words to it. The work of Steven Porges has
been instrumental in our understanding of our behaviours when we feel safe and
don't feel safe. He put forward Polyvagal Theory, a new way of understanding and
conceptualising how our autonomic nervous system (that is, the neural system in
our brain and spinal cord which is alert to danger) relates to our behaviour
(Porges, 2007). Porges' theory has been supported in research and practice.

Porges suggests that our autonomic nervous system is a system with three circuits. "The three circuits can be conceptualised as dynamic, providing adaptive
response to safe, dangerous, or life-threatening events or contexts" (Porges, 2007,
p. 120). The first circuit is called our social engagement system, which involves the
ventral vagal nerve. This nerve connects to the muscles in our face, larynx, pharynx, around our mouth, our heart and our lungs (Porges, 2007). When this
system is activated, we feel safe, we are open to possibilities, we can play, we can
learn, we can concentrate, our breathing and heart rate are steady. Kestly (2014)
conceptualises this as the "green light", where we are open to social engagement.
In order to learn in class, children need their social engagement system to be in a
state of activation.

When we do not feel safe, our defence systems are activated. Our second circuit
of response is the activation of our "flight or fight" system. This is our sympathetic
nervous system and when it is activated our social engagement system is

dampened down, our heart rate increases, we can't think clearly, we may panic and the adrenal gland is triggered to release cortisol (Kestly, 2014). The release of cortisol increases the body's capacity to handle stress and make more energy available (Nunn et al., 2008, p. 181). Hence, this system is called the "flight or fight" system as we want to run away fast or fight because of the sense of danger. The behaviours that may be observed in children when they are in this state could include: hyper vigilance, aggressive behaviour, hiding under tables, super busy, baby talk, overwhelmed, lashing out, agitation, and being argumentative. In this state, children cannot learn. Patriquin et al. (2019) concluded that autistic people exhibit a chronic autonomic nervous system response of hyperarousal where they perceive social situations are dangerous. This study highlights the importance of creating a sense of safety for autistic children, so they are not in a state of "fight of fight" (also see Chapter 11).

The next circuit of our defence system is when we feel under life threat. We are immobilised, we freeze. This is our dorsal motor nucleus of the vagal nerve (Porges, 2007). Children who have their dorsal vagal nerve activated are in hypoarousal (Kestly, 2014). They have reduced body movement, their breathing and heart rate has slowed down. An example of a child in this state would be a child who appears to be "like a deer in the headlights". Children cannot think when they are in this state, they can be confused, forgetful, not interested, not listening, and not learning. Claudio Mochi relates an example of children being in this frozen state during his work in Nigeria. He observed children frozen in their school class

> where their teachers were shouting and threatening them with a long bamboo stick to have their attention …. kids were humiliated just to make a point. Not a tangible threat there, but most of them [the children] felt so scared that they had zero chance to actively participate, learn and thrive properly. All they cared about was trying to protect themselves and finishing the class as soon as possible.
>
> (Mochi, 2022, p. 61)

When children are stressed, the brain expends more energy in protecting the self and being alert to possible threats (Kestly, 2014; Liu et al., 2017). This means the child is cognitively incapacitated, has few resources for long term planning, and is not learning (Kestly, 2014; Liu et al., 2017). The Australian Childhood Foundation has produced a Trauma Expression and Connection Assessment, for use by teachers to understand more fully the behaviour of children who show defensive responses because they do not feel safe (Australian Childhood Foundation, 2022).

Creating a sense of safety

Children perceive a sense of safety through neuroception (Geller & Porges, 2014; Porges, 2007). Neuroception occurs below our consciousness and is a neural process which constantly evaluates risk. It is triggered whenever we respond to safety (social engagement system), danger (flight and fight), or life threat (freeze) (Geller & Porges, 2014). Neuroception is bidirectional, which means a teacher and child's nervous systems are subconsciously monitoring the social situation between them (Geller & Porges, 2014).

A teacher can promote a sense of safety within the classroom, and hence activate children's social engagement system, through facial expressions such as smiling with the mouth and eyes, soothing vocal tones and steady rate of speaking, steady breathing and heart rate, open body posture and smooth movements (Geller & Porges, 2014). This is because the ventral vagal, our social engagement system, connects to facial muscles, larynx, pharynx, heart and lungs (see earlier). Activating children's social engagement system opens them to learning. As Haim Ginott (1972, p. 12) so astutely stated in relation to a teacher (italicised brackets added):

> It is my personal approach that creates the climate. It is my daily mood that makes the weather. I possess tremendous power to make a child's life miserable [*e.g. by invoking fear and punishmen*t] or joyous [*e.g. by being responsive, smiling, eye contact, calm rhythmic speaking*]. I can humiliate or humor, hurt or heal. My response decides whether a crisis will be escalated [*e.g. a child's flight or fight system is activated*] or de-escalated [*e.g. a child's social engagement system is activated*], and a child humanized or dehumanized.

Play, the brain, and learning

A neuroscientist called Jaak Panksepp devoted his life to researching the Mammalian Brain. His research uncovered seven motivational circuits or emotional systems that are intrinsic and genetic for all mammals, including humans (Panksepp & Biven, 2012; Kestly, 2014). Three circuits are active when we are connected to others. These are the circuits of CARE (nurturance), LUST (sexual excitement, relevant to adolescence), and PLAY (social joy). When we are out of connection with others, RAGE (anger), FEAR (anxiety), and PANIC/GRIEF (separation distress) are activated (Sunderland, 2007). SEEKING (expectancy) is connected to all these circuits and is active during PLAY. Panksepp referred to PLAY (social joy) as "one of the primary-process, genetically determined social urges" (Panksepp & Biven, 2012, p. 356). Children have a need to play.

PLAY circuits are organised in the Mammalian Brain (our Emotional Brain). These subcortical areas of the brain communicate with higher cortical areas (the Rational Brain), especially when children are engaged in symbolic or pretend play. For example, Whitehead et al. (2009) found many areas in the cortical and subcortical areas were activated when adults were watching objects used as symbols in play. Panksepp and Biven (2012) noted that "the primal urge to play is an important influence in helping program higher brain functions" (p. 365).

The PLAY circuit promotes social intelligence and as it is social joy (due to the widespread release of opioids and dopamine when it is activated), children can develop creative and positive ways of responding within their physical and social environments (Panksepp & Biven, 2012). A Learn to Play program was trialled in a special school (a school for children with IQs under 70) for 22 weeks with one group of children in their first year of school (O'Connor & Stagnitti, 2011). The children in the play group experienced increased time being involved in sensory-motor and pretend play experiences, while a comparison group did not spend time in play experiences (O'Connor & Stagnitti, 2011; Stagnitti et al., 2012). After 22 weeks it was found that the children who had experienced play were socially more connected compared to the non-play-curriculum group of children (O'Connor & Stagnitti, 2011). In this group of children, play made a positive impact on their social connections.

Experiences impact on brain development and "when children play, their activity promotes epigenetic changes" in the brain; for example, about 400 brain genes in the frontal cortical regions are modified by play (Panksepp & Biven, 2012, pp. 379, 380). Dynamic brain changes, evoked by play, facilitate and promote brain growth by creating pro-social circuits in the brain (Panksepp & Biven, 2012). Play helps develop the capacity in children to feel happy, self-reliant, and capable. It "helps to produce satisfied and self-actualised adults because it promotes emotional growth and social sensitivity" (Brown & Vaughan, 2009; Panksepp & Biven, 2012, p. 385).

Teachers have an important role in stimulating the SEEKING system of children, where learning becomes an anticipation and where a teacher can provide care and reassurance when a child experiences a sense of social loss (Panksepp & Biven 2012). Liu et al. (2017) and Zosh et al. (2017) provide evidence that guided play in the classroom is educational when it is joyful, meaningful, actively engaging, iterative, and socially interactive. This next section of the chapter looks at each of these aspects of play in relation to neuroscience and learning.

Joy

"Learning is emotional and associated with reward" (Liu et al., 2017, p. 6). Panksepp identified the PLAY circuit as social joy. The feeling of joy is motivational and is regulated in the subcortical limbic networks in our Mammalian Brain. These networks communicate constantly with higher order brain regions where processing of learning takes place (Liu et al., 2017). Experiencing joy is associated with increases in opioid and dopamine levels (involved in regulating reward, pleasure), which give us positive emotions (Liu et al., 2017). Dopamine tracts in the brain connect ancient subcortical levels of the brain with more evolutionary recent levels (prefrontal cortex/Rational Brain) (Liu et al., 2017; Panksepp & Biven, 2012). The positive effect of joy is linked to learning by increased attention and ability to process and retain information, working memory, flexibility in thinking, creativity, and improved stress regulation (Liu et al., 2017).

Meaningful

If what we are learning is not meaningful, we will not retain the information. When learning is meaningful, multiple networks are activated to make sense of new knowledge. This involves two neural networks (Liu et al., 2017). First, the fast-learning system network assists with rapid and focussed acquisition within a sense of safety. A second network at a later stage of learning puts the new knowledge into context so learning moves from effortful to automatic (Liu et al., 2017). An example of moving from effortful to automatic is analogical reasoning. Analogical reasoning is when a child makes connections between the known and unknown, for example, this thinking helps children see patterns or connections with prior knowledge (Liu et al., 2017).

When children can monitor themselves and self-regulate, they are showing ability in metacognition. This is because they are understanding their thought processes and understanding their abilities (Liu et al., 2017). Metacognition and self-regulation were effectively supported in a group of children engaged in pretend play in an educational setting compared to children in non-play educational settings (Whitebread et al., 2009). As children make meaning from new learning and understand their own thinking they also grow in confidence, which in turn prompts rewards from learning and improved memory retrieval (Liu et al., 2017). The hippocampus is in the Emotional Brain (Mammalian Brain), and it stores memories. There is stronger activity in the hippocampus when learning is rewarding and when new information is linked to known information in "aha" moments (Liu et al., 2017). In play, children can link known information with new information in a context that is meaningful to them. For example, a local school had a corner of the classroom dedicated to a play kitchen. A young boy, in his first year of school, would often play in this play space. Over several months he began to write "shopping lists" for what he needed in the "recipes" he was making in the play kitchen. His first written word was "apple juice", spelt phonetically. He was so proud and happy with this achievement that he went on to write more and more words on his "shopping list".

Actively engaging

Actively engaging is when a child is initiating actions and actively thinking about the learning at hand. This demands concentration, attention, and response. Academic skills are stimulated through effortful problem-solving and creativity, both of which can occur during children's self-initiation of pretend play, which involves a higher quality of thinking involving metacognitive and self-regulatory behaviours (Whitebread et al., 2009). "Neurally, active engagement is associated with networks involved in attention control, goal-directed behaviour, reward, temporal awareness, long term memory retrieval, and stress-regulation" (Liu et al., 2017, p. 14). The areas of the brain that are involved in these abilities are higher cognitive abilities found in the cortex (Liu, et al., 2017), or Rational Brain regions of the brain.

When adults were actively engaged in an activity where the challenge was dynamically adjusted to the participants' level of skill, it was found that the amygdala (the area of the emotional brain that is highly alert to threat) was low in activity (Ulrich et al., 2014). This indicates that being actively engaged in tasks or activities that are not overwhelming or boring, brings positive emotions that enhance our motivation to learn (Liu et al., 2017; Ulrich et al., 2014). Children who are actively engaged or self-initiating a task are able to inhibit distractions by sustaining focussed attention to a task (Liu et al., 2017).

Iterative

Iterative thinking is thinking that involves problem solving, and making and testing new hypotheses. The more we engage in iterative thinking, the more we are able to do it. Children who were engaged in pretend play were found to have iterative thinking because they were engaged in intentional learning, problem-solving, and creativity (Whitebread et al., 2009). At the neural level, iterative thinking involves cognitive processes such as perseverance, counterfactual reasoning, cognitive flexibility, and creativity or divergent problem solving (that is, there is more than one solution to a problem) (Liu et al., 2017). Chapter 6 discusses divergent problem solving in more depth.

Counterfactual reasoning is particularly relevant to pretend play because when children engage in object substitution (that is, using an object to symbolise something else in play, such as, a block for a mobile phone) they are using counterfactual reasoning (Zosh et al., 2017). Counterfactual reasoning involves keeping alternative options in our mind (for example, "I am talking into a block and the block is a phone"). This assists us to adapt to new information. Cognitive flexibility is also increased as children change their views and change their perspectives (Liu et al., 2017). Cognitive flexibility, divergent thinking, problem solving, and creativity are higher cognitive functions associated with the lateral prefrontal cortex, part of our Rational Brain (Liu et al., 2017).

Socially interactive

We are all social beings. A whole new area of study, called Interpersonal Neurobiology, has developed in the last decade on how the brain is shaped by social interaction (Siegel, 2012). Kestly (2014) wrote a book which applied this knowledge to play. Social pretend play is one of the most intellectually demanding activities of childhood because it demands reciprocal dialogue and reciprocal action between children (Whitebread & O'Sullivan, 2012, p. 200). During play, and particularly pretend play, children (if they wish to continue playing with peers), are constantly adjusting emotionally to the emotional needs of their peers, thinking beyond the literal about the ideas put forward by others as the play develops, and are using props and symbols in the play while also keeping track of character roles, solving problems, and negotiating resolutions (see Chapter 4). These metacognitive, meta-communicative, and self-regulatory abilities are strengthened during pretend play (Whitebread et al., 2009; Whitebread & O'Sullivan, 2012). Children not only need to perceive the intentions of others but also keep track of the meaning of the symbolic props in the play (for example, the block was a phone, but now it is a part of a railway track) (Rakoczy, 2008). This requires cognitive flexibility.

When children feel socially safe, learning in groups at school has shown benefits for critical thinking skills and language abilities (Zosh et al., 2017). Playing with others necessitates the ability to understand the perspectives of others, which might initiate processes such as theory of mind (taking another's perspective, see also Chapters 3, 4, and 5) (Liu et al., 2017). The ability to understand other's perspectives is integral for a child to benefit from learning in formal and informal teaching interactions (Liu et al., 2017).

An example of play in education

Children cannot learn when they are stressed. Earlier in this chapter was Claudio Mochi's description of his observation of children being in a state of "life threat" in schools in Nigeria. Mochi had been invited to the southern part of Nigeria by the Italian SOSolidarietà organisation in collaboration with a local partner and with the approval of the local government authorities. Italian SOSolidarietà had also observed that the children were well behaved, but they were apathetic, rigid, fearful, and experienced academic difficulties (Mochi & Stagnitti, 2023). Mochi's work was to bring to the community the "Developing Play Together" project.

This project began with Mochi and his team getting to know the teachers and training them in new ways of relating to children. Teachers had used punishment, didactic teaching, and rote learning. Mochi and his team trained teachers by introducing them to child-centred approaches along with the introduction of free play time for 30 minutes in their daily program (Mochi & Stagnitti, 2023). The classroom atmosphere began to change, with children being happy to come to school and teachers finding more satisfaction in their work.

With the introduction of free play activities, it became apparent to Mochi and his team that the children's play was experimental and exploratory, not symbolic or pretend play. The project then shifted to include knowledge of pretend play development using the Learn to Play approach (Stagnitti, 2021) in the teacher training. It took two more years for teachers to be trained and comfortable to include this new learning in their daily teaching (Mochi & Stagnitti, 2023). The subsequent shifts in the children were that they became socially engaged and were motivated to learn new knowledge (Mochi & Stagnitti, 2023). Children were actively engaged in learning. They experienced joy, meaningfulness in learning and added new knowledge as their iterative thinking and counterfactual thinking increased. The project lasted for five years, after which time it became too dangerous to travel to Nigeria (Mochi & Stagnitti, 2023). However, because the training had included training teachers to be trainers, the work could continue in the schools.

The example from Nigeria shows the five characteristics of playful learning in the children's responses. This shift in the children's joy and motivation to learn was "associated with neural networks involved in brain processes including reward, memory, cognitive flexibility, and stress regulation that are activated during learning" (Liu et al., 2017, p. 20). A child who has developed pathways and constant communication between the Reptilian, Mammalian, and Rational Brain is a child whose brain is integrating, which means the child has more control of their emotions, can self-regulate, and use metacognitive and metacommunication abilities. Part of the integration of a child's brain also includes integration of the right and left hemispheres (or sides) of the brain (Siegel & Bryson, 2012). The next section looks at this integration with the example of narrative.

Narrative, play, and the brain

Narrative in this chapter refers to storytelling. "Narrative is a complex cognitive task and involves social-perceptual theory of mind" where children co-construct the story when playing with others (Rakoczy, 2008; Stagnitti, 2016, p. 54).

> For example, producing a narrative involves relating a set of events which are sequentially organised in time and space, cause and effect, an evaluative point, global structure, different perspectives of characters and psychological states, and for some narratives, a narrator's voice (Stirling et al., 2014).
>
> (Stagnitti, 2016, p. 54)

Narratives are critical to learning, as understanding narratives is involved in story comprehension and literacy tasks.

Narrative development and pretend play development parallel and dovetail with each other. For example, at 2 years of age, children play out life events they have experienced in and out of the home and in oral narratives; they can tell a story about themselves (Stagnitti & Jellie, 2023). These early play experiences contribute to a child's autobiographical narrative, that is, a story about themselves – a felt sense of what they do and an emerging sense of self. Through play children explore an understanding of themselves and the world around them. From 3 to 5 years, children shift from descriptions of objects to temporal sequencing of events relevant to solving a problem, and in their play they can create long stories that reflect their life, or fictional stories with problems and resolutions (Stagnitti & Jellie, 2023). Children continue to develop an understanding of the self in this process, with autobiographical narrative giving them a sense of identity.

The ability to tell or listen to a narrative integrates the right and left sides of the brain (Siegel & Bryson, 2012) because it integrates words with emotions. The left side of the brain desires order; it is logical, literal, and linguistic and makes sense of, and provides words for, our feelings and memories (Siegel & Bryson, 2012). The left side processes rules of grammar, facts, categorises, abstracts and unpacks our experiences with words (Kestly, 2014). The right side of our brain picks up non-verbal interactions (such as facial expressions, eye contact, tone of voice, gesture) and processes emotions and information about our sense of self. It takes in the big picture and the meaning and feel of an experience; it is intuitive (Siegel & Bryson, 2012). The right-side processes new experiences, deals with ambiguity, and creates embodied implicit memories (Kestly, 2014). When we are processing narratives, the right hemisphere processes non-verbal storytelling, and makes sense of the whole including sounds and feelings. This information is sent to the left hemisphere where the experience is expressed in language, which is re-presented to the right hemisphere in language. The right hemisphere then processes the "feeling" of the narrative and words into metaphorical information which gives us a coherent story (Kestly, 2014). The process of right-left-right continues to give us "a sense of the meaning of the story in our bodies while hearing the story told in words" (Kestly, 2014, p. 121).

The development of pretend play and narrative were examined in a longitudinal study over 6 months by Stagnitti et al. (2016), who independently measured vocabulary, grammar, quality of pretend play ability, narrative re-tell, and social competence among 54 children from three schools. One school had play embedded in the curriculum through guided play activities and free play at recess breaks. Two schools had a traditional curriculum with set times for subjects and no play activities embedded in the classroom. After 6 months, it was found that the children with the play-based curriculum showed a significantly greater growth in narrative re-tell ability and grammatical knowledge than children in the traditional curriculum. This study provided evidence that play-based instruction is associated with significant growth in narrative ability across the first 6 months of formal learning.

Conclusion

A child's brain is experience dependent, therefore schooling and the teacher–child relationship can impact on the development of children's brains and their learning. By creating a feeling of safety within the classroom and the school, a child's social engagement system can be activated, and defence systems dampened down. This provides an environment where a child is open to learning. When guided play is introduced into the classroom the characteristics of joyful, meaningful learning can occur because many brain functions are activated and integrated. Iterative thought processes and children actively engaged in learning and social interaction activate areas of the brain with functions related to memory, reward, cognitive flexibility, and self-regulation. This activation involves pathways communicating between the social-emotional areas and the higher functioning cognitive processing areas of the brain. Right–left connections in the brain were discussed in relation to narrative ability. Children function at their best when they are settled, calm, and there is integration between the lower–higher and right–left sides of the brain. A child can then experience the joy and rewards of learning.

References

Allison, K. L., & Rossouw, P. J. (2013). The therapeutic alliance: Exploring the concept of "safety" from a neuropsychotherapeutic perspective. *International Journal of Neuropsychotherapy*, 1, 21–29. doi:10.12744/ijnpt.2013.0021-0029.

Australian Childhood Foundation (2022). TECA: Trauma Expression and Connection Assessment. Melbourne. https://professionals.childhood.org.au/resources/.

Brown, S. & Vaughan, C. (2009). *Play: How it shapes the brain, opens the imagination, and invigorates the soul.* Penguin.

Geller, S. M. & Porges, S.W. (2014). Therapeutic presence: Neurophysiological mechanisms mediating feeling safe in therapeutic relationships. *Journal of Psychotherapy Integration*, 24, 178–192. doi:10.1037/a0037511.

Ginott, H. (1972). *Teacher and child: A book for parents and teachers.* Macmillan.

Kestly, T. (2014). *The interpersonal neurobiology of play: Brain-building interventions for emotional well-being.* W.W. Norton.

Liu, C. S., Solis, L., Jensen, H., Hopkins, E., Neale, D., Zosh, J., Hirsh-Pasek, K. & Whitebread, D. (2017). *Neuroscience and learning through play: A review of the evidence.* The LEGO Foundation.

Mochi, C. (2022). *Beyond the clouds. An autoethnographic research exploring good practice in crisis settings.* Loving Healing Press.

Mochi, C. & Stagnitti, K. (2023). Learn to Play therapy in high-risk countries: The example of Nigeria. In I. Cassina, C. Mochi, & K. Stagnitti (Eds.), *Play therapy and expressive arts in a complex and dynamic world: Opportunities and challenges inside and outside the playroom* (pp. 96–119). Routledge.

Nunn, K., Hanstock, T., & Lask, B. (2008). *Who's who of the brain. A guide to its inhabitants, where they live and what they do.* Jessica Kingsley.

O'Connor, C. & Stagnitti, K. (2011). Play, behaviour, language and social skills: The comparison of a play and a non-play intervention within a specialist school setting. *Research in Developmental Disabilities*, 32, 1205–1211. doi:10.1016/j.ridd.2010.12.037.

Patriquin, M., Hartwig, E., Friedman, B., Porges, S., & Scarpa, A. (2019). Autonomic response in autism spectrum disorder: Relationship to social and cognitive functioning. *Biological Psychology*, 145, 185–197. doi:10.1016/j.biopsycho.2019.05.004.

Panksepp, J., & Biven, L. (2012). *The archaeology of mind: Neuroevolutionary origins of human emotions.* W.W. Norton.

Porges, S. W. (2007). The polyvagal perspective. *Biological Psychology*, 74, 116–143. doi:10.1016/j.biopsycho.2006.06.009.

Rakoczy, H. (2008). Pretense as individual and collective intentionality. *Mind & Language*, 23(5), 499–517. doi:10.1111/j.1468–0017.2008.00357.x.

Siegel, D. (2012). *The developing mind: How relationships and the brain interact to shape who we are* (2nd edn). Guilford Press.

Siegel, D., & Bryson, T. (2012). *The whole-brain child.* Bantam Books.

Stagnitti, K. (2021). *Learn to Play therapy: Principles, processes and practical activities.* Learn to Play.

Stagnitti, K. (2016). Play, narrative, and children with Autism. In S. Douglas & L. Stirling (Eds.), *Children's play, pretence, and story: Studies in culture, context, and autism spectrum disorder* (pp. 51–71). Psychology Press.

Stagnitti, K., Bailey, A., Hudspbeth-Stevenson, E., Reynolds, R., & Kidd, E. (2016). An investigation into the effect of play-based instruction on the development of play skills and oral language: A 6-month longitudinal study. *Journal of Early Childhood Research*, 14(4), 389–406. doi:10.1177/1476718X15579741.

Stagnitti, K. & Jellie, L. (2023). Play and storytelling: Building literacy skills in the early years. Learn to Play. www.learntoplayevents.com.

Stagnitti, K., O'Connor, C., & Sheppard, L. (2012). The impact of the Learn to Play program on play, social competence and language for children aged 5–8 years who attend a special school. *Australian Occupational Therapy Journal*, 59(4), 302–311. doi:10.1111/j.1440–1630.2012.01018.x.

Stirling, L., Douglas, S., Leekam, S. & Carey, L. (2014). The use of narrative in studying communication in Autism Spectrum Disorders. In J. Arciuli and J. Brock (Eds.), *Communication in autism* (pp. 171–215). John Benjamins.

Sunderland, M. (2007). *What every parent needs to know.* DK Books.

Ulrich, M., Ketter, J., Hoenig, K., Waller, C., & Grön, G. (2014). Neural correlates of experimentally induced flow experiences. *Neuroimage*, 86, 194–202. doi:10.1016/j.neuroimage.2013.08.019.

Whitebread, D., Coltman, P., Jameson, H., & Lander, R. (2009). Play, cognition and self-regulation: What exactly are children learning when they learn through play? *Educational & Child Psychology*, 26, 40–52.

Whitebread, D., & O'Sullivan, L. (2012). Preschool children's social pretend play: Supporting the development of metacommunication, metacognition, and self-regulation. *International Journal of Play*, 1, 197–213. doi:10.1080/21594937.2012.693384.

Whitehead, C., Marchant, J. L., Craik, D., & Firth, C. D. (2009). Neural correlates of observing pretend play in which one object is represented as another. *Social Cognitive Affective Neuroscience*, 4, 369–378. doi:10.1093/scan/nsp021.

Zosh, J. M., Hopkins, E. J., Jensen, H., Liu, C., Neale, D., Hirsh-Pasek, K., Solis, S. L., & Whitebread, D. (2017). *Learning through play: A review of the evidence*. White paper. LEGO Foundation. https://cms.learningthroughplay.com/media/wmtlmbe0/learning-through-play_web.pdf.

3 Communication, Language, and Pretend Play

Communication is part of our everyday lives and involves many cognitive and interactive processes that support us to convey our thoughts, ideas, needs, and desires to others. Communication may be in verbal (spoken), non-verbal (gestural, tone, pitch, etc.) or written forms, whereby two or more people co-construct shared meaning and understandings (McLeod & McCormack, 2015; Paatsch & Nolan, 2020). In any communicative exchange, typically there is a speaker and a listener. The speaker must formulate their thoughts and ideas and encode these into language to convey to their conversational partner, the listener. For example, a child who is hungry and would like a biscuit to eat may formulate this request using words "I'm hungry, can I please have a biscuit?" They may also accompany this request using non-verbal aspects of language such as pointing to the biscuit or smiling when they say "please". Once receiving this message, the listener must decode the message, interpret the intended meaning, and formulate their response to the speaker prior to taking their turn. As both partners in the conversation take their turns, they take on the role of speaker and listener throughout the exchange. They use and interpret the verbal and non-verbal aspects of the language, including words, sentences, and phrases, as well as body language, eye gaze, facial expressions, pitch, duration, and intensity.

Language is a set of complex symbols and involves mastering the rules for combining these symbols to communicate with others. To become an effective language user, we develop both the expressive and receptive forms. Receptive language involves listening and watching the language used by others, while expressive language refers to the productive form of language including verbal, sign, and non-verbal cues. Language develops within socially interactive environments where adults, particularly family members, caregivers, and teachers, play a critical role in supporting young children's language development as they engage in rich, abundant talk throughout everyday routines and activities.

Language can be divided into three major components: *Form, Content,* and *Use* (Bloom and Lahey, 1978; Owens, 2016). All components are interrelated and include five subsystems of language: *syntax, morphology, phonology, semantics,* and *pragmatics. Form* involves the understanding and use of skills related to the structure of phrases and sentences (syntax), words including prefixes, plurals, suffixes to mark meaning (morphology), and sounds including how they are made,

DOI: 10.4324/9781003296782-4

sequenced, and distributed (phonology). *Content* includes the understanding and use of words and word combinations, and the ability to retain and retrieve words to make sense of what is being said (semantics). *Use* is the social use of language (pragmatics) related to many aspects of cognitive development including social and emotional, and theory of mind (see Chapter 4 for more information on the latter). Pragmatics involve understanding and using the rules for carrying out cooperative conversations, including skills to: take turns, repair exchanges in conversations when they have broken down, use appropriate eye contact, be contingent on one's partner's contributions, initiate and maintain topics, use pausing, and use the other subsystems of language to "arrive at *what can or must be said* in order to get across *what is meant* and to arrive at *what is meant* on the basis of *what is said*" (Schmid & Schmid, 2012, p. 3). In addition, pragmatic language development is closely linked to narrative as children build stories with a central focus, problem, and resolution (Paul, 2007). To develop language, young children need to be provided with opportunities to engage in many interactions with a variety of partners across different social contexts. One rich context for supporting language acquisition is pretend play.

Let's now look at an example from the context of the classroom. Two foundation children, Sophia and Eliza, are playing in the café that the teacher has set up in the classroom. The following excerpt presents the exchange between the two girls at the beginning of the play session as they negotiate their roles prior to starting the play.

SOPHIA: [looking at Eliza] OK, I will be the café lady who asks you what you want to eat. You can come in and buy a coffee and two cakes. You sit here [points to the chair]. OK? [rising inflection and smiles]

ELIZA: [looking at Sophia] OK, but I don't want two cakes and I want a milkshake. What's the name of the café?

In this short exchange both girls are using all the subsystems of language to communicate their ideas, needs and desires. They can formulate their words into sentences (syntax), add the /s/ in the word cakes to mark more than one (morphology), and sequence, distribute, and produce the sounds within the words (phonology). Both girls have a variety of word types including pronouns (I, you), nouns, (café, lady, cakes, coffee), conjunctions (and) and verbs (want, will be, sit). The girls also demonstrate several sophisticated pragmatic skills within the social context of the interaction. For example, Sophia initiates the conversation marking it with "OK" and using eye contact to engage her partner. She is directive in communicating her need to be the "café lady" and the role she wants Eliza to play ("I will", "you want", "you can", "you sit"). However, she also manipulates her language by ending her utterance with "OK" and the use of a smile, understanding the need to convince Eliza that her idea is accepted. Eliza takes her turn by agreeing that Sophia's plan was "OK". She is also contingent on her partner's contribution to the exchange by maintaining (responds to Sophia's question, "OK?") and extending the topic ("What's the name of the café?"). Eliza also shows her ability to disagree with Sophia's plan and negotiates the details with her regarding what to order ("don't want two cakes and I want a milkshake"). Together the girls co-construct the play scene using verbal and non-verbal language. Such pretend play contexts support a developing sense of self within collaborative dialogues, social competencies and acceptance, and build friendships.

Link between language and play

Play, particularly pretend play, shares many conceptual similarities with language in that both are symbolic and rely on communication within social contexts (Creaghe & Kidd, 2022; Creaghe et al., 2021; Quinn et al., 2018). As discussed in Chapter 1 in this book, pretend play, while complex and often difficult to define, includes many characteristics such as the ability to: impose meaning on actions, objects and toys; substitute objects; attribute imagined properties to objects; refer to absent objects in the play; sustain thinking; understand characters and motivations; and sequence play actions logically (Creaghe et al., 2021; Reynolds et al., 2011; Stagnitti, 2004).

Pretend play and language acquisition have long been linked (Creaghe, 2020; Creaghe et al., 2021; Christie & Roskos, 2006; Hirsh-Pasek et al., 2009; Lillard et al., 2013; Zigler et al., 2004). In play, children imitate behaviours from their real-life contexts (McCune, 1995) or create role-play in a fantasy world. In the early years of life, children will often use sound effects, gestures, and facial expressions to accompany their actions (McCune, 1995) and as their play becomes more complex, they start to use more complex symbolic language (Campbell et al., 2018; Vygotsky, 1967; 1978). Pretend play provides children with opportunities to use language to tell their story and to engage in pretence. As such, children are immersed in a rich environment that enables them to be creative in both producing and developing language (Hà, 2022).

Research has shown that aspects of pretend play also predict children's language development. For example, a recent study by Stagnitti et al. (2020) investigated the pretend play and oral language abilities of a group of 30 children at the commencement of their first year of schooling. Results showed that the child's ability to symbolise and use an object for something else in the play predicted a child's overall receptive and expressive language abilities. Similarly, Kizildere et al. (2020) examined the links between pretend play and language in 119 pre-schoolers in Turkey and found that earlier pretend play skills, measured at 4 years of age, predicted these children's later receptive language at the age of 5 years. Research has also shown that pretend play and language skills develop concurrently and are closely related in development (Bergen, 2002; Quinn et al., 2018). Quinn et al. (2018) conducted a review of the literature and concluded that together, these studies demonstrated a strong relationship between pretend play and language development, placing no doubt on the relationship between pretend play and language. McCune (1995) tested the hypotheses on the relationship between pretend play and language development in a longitudinal study with six children (3 female and 3 male) aged between 9 and 24 months and found that children made language gains at the same time as equivalent play developments, thus providing further evidence to support the relationship between pretend play and language development.

In addition to the studies that have examined the link between pretend play and broad measures of language, there is also a large body of research that has examined the links between pretend play and the specific components of language (*Form, Content,* and *Use*). In the following sections of this chapter, we present a review of this research to demonstrate the strong link between pretend play and the specific components of language.

Form of language and play

As discussed, *Form* includes syntax, morphology, and phonology. Research has shown that there is a link between pretend play and children's syntactic development. For example, Creaghe et al. (2021) found that conversational turns in symbolic [also known as pretend] play predicted grammatical knowledge, as measured by children's Mean Length of Utterance at 18 months and 24 months. In an earlier study, Casby and Corte (1987) found that children who were able to sequence two or more pretend play behaviours or who could substitute objects were also able to produce words in combination (i.e., syntax). Similarly, Fekonja et al. (2005) found that the 60 children aged 4 to 5 years in their study produced more complex syntactic language such as multi-word utterances and interrogative clauses (e.g., questions such as "What are you doing?" "Can I be the doctor?") than when in routine and guided activities, such as maths.

Other studies comparing children's language development in classrooms using a play-based approach with classrooms using a more traditional school curricula are also evident in the research literature. For example, Stagnitti et al. (2016) compared linguistic development in a group of 54 school-aged children in their first year of schooling in two different contexts: (1) a classroom with play-based curricula, and (2) a traditional didactic and directed classroom environment. Results of children's performances on the Test for Reception of Grammar – 2 (Bishop, 2003) showed improvements in grammatical knowledge in both contexts; however, students in the play-based program showed greater improvement than children in the more traditional didactic environment.

There are limited studies that have investigated the link between pretend play and phonological development. However, Orr and Geva (2015) found that the age of initiation of single-object pretend play correlates with the age of initiation of later-emerging vocal outputs, suggesting the strong link between language production and pretend play. Christie and Roskos (2006) also suggest that sounds represent different objects and components of the play as children act out stories and engage in pretend play using language. Such findings also suggest the strong link between play, language, and early literacy skills where children begin to understand the use of sounds in communicating in spoken and written form. For example, let's go back to the scene when Sophia and Eliza were playing in the café. Once the roles were established the play continued. Eliza sat at the table and waited for Sophia to come and take her order. Eliza ordered her chocolate milk-shake and cake. Sophia started to write Eliza's order on a piece of paper and vocalised the words as she wrote. She wrote "1 choklet milcshayc and 1 strorbry cayc". In this example, it is clear that Sophia has an understanding of both the production of sounds and their relationship to the orthographical representations in writing.

Content of language and play

Play also provides a rich environment to support children's semantic development as they hear and use words within different pretend play contexts (café, super-market, home corner, dress-ups). In a recent study by Creaghe et al. (2021), results showed that conversational turns in symbolic play positively correlated with infants' gesture use and vocabulary comprehension and production. In particular, when caregivers used mimetics (i.e., word forms or sounds that mimic and/or symbolise the sound associated with the object or pretence sound – e.g., meow, woof, brrrm, woosh), infants were drawn into the context of communicative actions. Such findings are also evident in our own observations of young children's play in the primary school classroom. Let's return to the example of Sophia and Eliza at the café. As their play progressed, Sophia extended her role as waitress to include the cook who made the milkshake and selected the cake to put on the plate. As she made the milkshake, she made noises of the pretend machine (a box with a stick) as it mixed the milk with the chocolate sauce. She also made a "plop" noise as she added ice-cream to the glass. During this scene, Sophia narrated what she was doing, saying "I'm going to mix the milk and chocolate and I'll add two ice-creams." Eliza watched and listened to Sophia, engaging in the play with her friend. Both girls demonstrated joint attention both with each other and with the object as they co-constructed the narrative, suggesting that both girls were drawn into the context of this rich communicative exchange.

Research has also shown that there is a strong link between pretend play and semantic problem solving (Bergen, 2002) and pretend play and vocabulary growth. For example, Han et al. (2010), found that four- and five-year-old chil-dren from low-income families who received vocabulary intervention within a play environment showed more growth in receptive and expressive vocabulary com-pared with the children who were not in the play context. In addition, these chil-dren showed an increased performance trajectory in vocabulary learning, suggesting the importance of play for supporting vocabulary development – a cri-tical component for early literacy and reading comprehension.

Further studies have shown the strong link between the level of complexity of children's pretend play and their semantic development. For example, Melzer and Palermo (2016) found that Mean Length of Utterance and children's use of mental state words (want, wish, think, love, happy, excited, think, know, etc.) were related to increased pretend play complexity in typically developing three- and four-year-old children. Similarly, Stagnitti and Lewis (2015) found that aspects of pretend play (when children were in preschool) were predictive of children's semantic abilities four years later. Specifically, they found that elaborate play, which included the use of symbols in play and logical sequences of action, predicted the child's semantic organisation abilities such as understanding that objects may share specific features and attributes, and may be organised according to a particular function and/or category. For example, the function of many objects may be to support eating (e.g., cup, spoon, knife, etc.) but may be further divided into categories such as those used to cut food or those made from the same materials (e.g., metal, plastic, etc.). The children who were able to sequence their play in a series of logical actions, such as picking up the teddy, feeding the teddy a drink, putting the teddy to bed, and covering the teddy with a blanket were predictive of their semantic abilities when they were 8 or 9 years old.

Again, let's return to Sophia and Eliza at the café. The following excerpt from their play demonstrates the ways in which the pretend play context supported their vocabulary use as well as their use of logical sequence of actions.

SOPHIA: [Moves to the café table to take Eliza's order. She is holding a small pad of paper and pen and looks at Eliza to take her order] Hello, are you ready, can I take your order please?

ELIZA: [Pause. Eliza looks puzzled] What's an order?

SOPHIA: You know, tell me what you want.

ELIZA: Oh OK, Can I have a chocolate milkshake and a red cake.

SOPHIA: [Writing the order on her paper] OK, one chocolate milkshake and one strawberry cake. I will be back soon.

ELIZA: Thank you. [She picks up a block and pretends it is her phone, scrolling through the apps].

This excerpt shows the ways in which Sophia supported Eliza's vocabulary by explaining the word "order" and expanding her description of "red" to introduce the word "strawberry". Together, they expanded their script to include a series of logical actions, involving the sequence of taking an order before bringing the food to the table.

Use of language and play

As we have discussed throughout this book, pretend play requires the ability to represent objects and actions symbolically, and is carried out through narration, social conversation, and negotiation between peers (Bergen, 2002). Pretend play places high linguistic demands on children to use language within various social contexts with a range of partners. Children must talk about what is happening in the play, identify and elaborate on play themes, negotiate and take turns with their partners in the play, and respond throughout the play (Christie & Roskos, 2006). Similarly, language acquisition occurs within rich social contexts (Creaghe, 2020) as children interact with others in their environment. Such skills and abilities are strongly linked to children's pragmatic language – the social use of language (Paatsch & Toe, 2020). Pragmatics skills are also important to the development of the complex cognitive processes that are required to engage in conversation, supporting the strong link between pragmatics, social and emotional development, and pretend play, highlighting the importance of social interaction in children's development. As such, pretend play provides a rich context for children to use language socially and to develop pragmatic skills such as turn-taking, initiation, taking the perspective of another, and building narrative.

Fekonja et al. (2005) found that the 60 four- and five-year-old children in their study engaged in rich dialogue with each other during play, particularly as the children established the rules of the game and distributed and adopted roles. They suggested that role playing and the use of various objects with a different function from that which they have in the real world are critical for children's language development. In pretend play, children are required to symbolically transform their verbal expression in order to make it understandable to their peers, suggesting that children need to take the perspective of others during the play – an ability that is linked to the social use of language (pragmatics) and theory of mind (see also Chapters 4 and 5).

Research has also shown that particular pragmatic skills, such as topic initiation, are linked to pretend play. For example, Melzer and Palermo (2016) found that children who initiated play more frequently were more likely to exhibit complex pretend play behaviours than those who initiated less frequently. These findings suggest that children's ability to initiate play may also support children's pragmatic skills, particularly their ability to initiate topics with others. For example, if we return to the first excerpt between Sophia and Eliza as they established their roles in the café scene, it is evident that Sophia not only initiated the play but also initiated the topic of ordering food at a café. Together, these forms of initiation support play and language abilities, strengthening the social domain of the girls' development as they interact with each other and co-construct their play scripts.

Pretend play also provides opportunities for children to use metacommunication to establish their roles, plan and extend the play, and build narrative. For example, children communicate the roles (e.g., "I will be the shopkeeper and you can be the customer") and the setting and plot (e.g., "We are in a toy shop, and you are going to buy some Lego … but I don't have the one you want"), often requiring perspective taking and negotiation. In a recent study by de Haan et al. (2021), who investigated metacommunication skills of 24 Dutch children aged 5 years during pretend play, findings showed that there is a positive relationship between children's narrative in pretend play and their use of metacommunication as they negotiate and cooperate with their peers in the social context (see Chapter 5 for more discussion on metacommunication).

Similar findings related to the relationship between play and children's narrative abilities have been widely reported in the literature. Ilgaz and Aksu-Koç (2005) found that pretend play contexts supported young 3-, 4-, and 5-year-old Turkish children's narrative abilities. Specifically, children's narratives, consisting of sequences of temporal-causal events that typically include setting/s, characters, problems, and resolutions, were enhanced in the play context compared to non-play contexts. Stagnitti et al. (2016) also found that children in their first year of school who participated in a play-based program where the environment was set up with play spaces, showed significant growth in their narrative skills compared with the children who did not attend a play-based program. These narrative abilities were also significantly associated with their growth in play abilities, suggesting that "play and narrative are complementary expressions of children's symbolic imagination" (p. 401). Similarly, Stagnitti and Lewis (2015) found that a child's ability to substitute objects in their play (e.g., a block for a phone) predicted later narrative re-telling abilities in this group of children. In a later study by Stagnitti et al. (2020) results showed a significant relationship between children's narrative scores, as measured by story content and ideas, and object substitution. In a more recent study that explored the connection between children's play and story creativity in a group of 151 4- to 6-year-old European-American children, findings showed that children who incorporated more props and plots in their stories engaged more in pretend play, suggesting that children who construct creative narratives are also using these same skills when developing their pretend play scripts (Holmes et al., 2022). Further findings from this study showed that children who engage in group cooperative pretend play construct more creative narratives than those children who engage in solitary play, suggesting that play narratives support children's story creation, "and the added interaction between peers during social pretend play can be even more beneficial to children's story making skills" (Holmes et al., 2022, p. 10) (see Chapter 6 for more discussion on creative thinking and storytelling).

The importance of children playing with others is also highlighted by Zosh et al. (2022), who suggest that peer interactions during play provide children with opportunities to be contingent on other's contributions, to ask and answer questions, argue and defend a position, and to construct new shared knowledge. Together, these findings support the argument that pretend play is a rich context for supporting children' pragmatic language abilities, and building social and self-regulatory skills (see also Chapters 4 and 5).

Let's return to Sophia and Eliza as they build their pretend play narrative in the café to demonstrate how pretend play supports pragmatic skills including turn-taking, contingency, repair, perspective taking, narrative, and social skills. The following excerpt presents another section of their exchange later in their play.

SOPHIA: [Bringing the milkshake and cake to the table] Here is your milkshake and cake.

ELIZA: Thank you. [Looks at the cake] This is a brown cake not strawberry.

SOPHIA: Oh sorry I will get you a strawberry cake. [Goes back and changes the round brown block to a red block]

ELIZA: [Eats the cake then goes to the counter to pay. She uses her phone to pay for the food and looks for the machine to pay. At this stage, there is no machine, so she looks around] Where do I pay?

SOPHIA: Hmm. [Looks away and there is a long pause of 4 seconds].

ELIZA: Where do I pay? Do you have a thing to swipe my phone to pay … you know?

SOPHIA: Ohhhh sorry, our machine is broken but here is a new one. [She looks around and pick up a small box and puts it on the counter] I hope it works. Tap here.

This excerpt demonstrates the use of sophisticated pragmatic skills by both girls as they co-construct their narrative. They take turns through a series of statements (e.g., "Here is your milkshake and cake"; "I hope it works", "Tap here"); questions (e.g., "Where do I pay?"); and responses (e.g., "our machine is broken but here is a new one"). Eliza introduces several problems to the narrative by stating that she has received the wrong cake and that there is nowhere to pay for her food. Both problems are quickly resolved by Sophia. There is also evidence of breakdown and repair in the conversation. For example, it is clear that Sophia is not completely sure of what Eliza is referring to when she asks, "Where do I pay?" This is followed by a lengthy pause and a change in eye contact. However, Eliza is aware of the need to repair this breakdown and self-repairs by repeating the question then provides more information to clarify her requests to ensure that the conversation and narrative continue. Both Sophia and Eliza also appear to take the perspective of the other. For example, Eliza is aware that Sophia has not understood her and is required to repair the misunderstanding. Sophia is aware that Eliza is looking for something to use in the play so that she can use her phone to pay for the food and responds by quickly finding something to ensure that Eliza's needs are met and that the play can continue. Together, the use of these pragmatic skills within the play context supports the argument for the strong link between narrative, play, and the social use of language.

Conclusion

There is a large body of research that has linked pretend play with many components of language development, including form, content, and use. In this chapter we have highlighted the interconnectedness between these language components and pretend play skills such as object substitution, play scripts, sequences of play action, and role play. We have provided some examples from children's play scripts as they engage in pretend play in the primary school classroom to highlight the ways in which pretend play can provide a rich context for language acquisition, including the social use of language. Teachers play a critical role in setting up these rich play contexts to support children's learning within social interactions with others including peers, teachers, education support officers, and parents. We argue that these important contexts provide a fertile environment for optimising learning across many domains including the cognitive, the social and emotional, and the linguistic, and support children to be engaged in authentic, interactive, and meaningful experiences.

References

Bergen, D. (2002). The role of pretend play in children's cognitive development. *Early Childhood Research & Practice*, 4(1), n1.

Bishop, D. V. M. (2003). *Test for reception of grammar* (2nd edn). Pearson Education.

Bloom, L., & Lahey, M. (1978). *Language development and language disorders.* Monograph. Columbia University.

Campbell, S. B., Mahoney, A. S., Northrup, J., Moore, E. L., Leezenbaum, N. B., & Brownell, C. A. (2018). Developmental changes in pretend play from 22- to 34-months in younger siblings of children with autism spectrum disorder. *Journal of abnormal child psychology*, 46, 639–654. doi:10.1007/s10802-017-0324-3.

Casby, M. W. & Corte, M. D. (1987). Symbolic play performance and early language development. *Journal of Psycholinguistic Research*, 16, 31–42.

Christie, J. F. & Roskos, K. A. (2006). Standards, science, and the role of play in early literacy education. In D. Singer., R. Golinkoff, & K. Hirsh-Pasek (Eds.), *Play = learning: How play motivates and enhances children's cognitive and social-emotional growth* (pp. 57–73). Oxford University Press.

Creaghe, N. V. (2020). Symbolic play and language acquisition: The dynamics of infant-caretaker communication during symbolic play. Unpublished doctoral dissertation, The Australian National University, Australia.

Creaghe, N., & Kidd, E. (2022). Symbolic play as a zone of proximal development: An analysis of informational exchange. *Social Development*, 31(4), 1138–1156. doi:10.1111.sode.12592.

Creaghe, N., Quinn, S., & Kidd, E. (2021). Symbolic play provides a fertile context for language development. *Infancy*, 26(6), 980–1010. doi:10.1111.infa.12422.

de Haan, D., Vriens-van Hoogdalem, A. G., Zeijlmans, K., & Boom, J. (2021). Meta-communication in social pretend play: Two dimensions. *International Journal of Early Years Education*, 29(4), 405–419. doi:10.1080/09669760.2020.1778451.

Fekonja, U., Umek, L. M., & Kranjc, S. (2005). Free play and other daily preschool activities as a context for child's language development. *Studia psychologica*, 47(2), 103.

Hà, T. A. (2022). Pretend play and early language development – relationships and impacts: A comprehensive literature review. *Journal of Education*, 202(1), 122–130. doi:10.1177/0022057420966761.

Han, M., Moore, N., Vukelich, C., & Buell, M. (2010). Does play make a difference? How play intervention affects the vocabulary learning of at-risk preschoolers. *American Journal of Play*, 3(1), 82–105.

Hirsh-Pasek, K., Golinkoff, R. M., Berk, L. E., & Singer, D. (2009). *A mandate for playful learning in preschool: Applying the scientific evidence.* Oxford University Press. doi:10.1093/acprof:oso/9780195382716.001.0001.

Holmes, R. M., Kohm, K., Genise, S., Koolidge, L., Mendelson, D., Romeo, L., & Bant, C. (2022). Is there a connection between children's language skills, creativity, and play? *Early Child Development and Care*, 192(8), 1178–1189. doi:10.1080/03004430.2020.1853115.

Ilgaz, H., & Aksu-Koç, A. (2005). Episodic development in preschool children's play: Prompted and direct-elicited narratives. *Cognitive Development*, 20(4), 526–544. doi:10.1016/j.cogdev.2005.08.004.

Kızıldere, E., Aktan-Erciyes, A., Tahiroğlu, D., & Göksun, T. (2020). A multidimensional investigation of pretend play and language competence: Concurrent and longitudinal relations in preschoolers. *Cognitive Development*, 54, 100870. doi:10.1016/j.cogdev.2020.100870.

Lillard, A. S., Lerner, M. D., Hopkins, E. J., Dore, R. A., Smith, E. D., & Palmquist, C. M. (2013). The impact of pretend play on children's development: A review of the evidence. *Psychological Bulletin*, 139(1), 1. doi:10.1037/a0029321.

McLeod, S., & McCormack, J. (2015). *Introduction to speech, language and literacy.* Oxford University Press.

McCune, L. (1995). A normative study of representational play in the transition to language. *Developmental psychology*, 31(2), 198.

Melzer, D. K., & Palermo, C. A. (2016). "Mommy, you are the princess and I am the queen": How preschool children's initiation and language use during pretend play relate to complexity. *Infant and Child Development*, 25(2), 221–230. doi:10.1002/icd.1927.

Orr, E., & Geva, R. (2015). Symbolic play and language development. *Infant Behavior and Development*, 38, 147–161. doi:10.1016/j.infbeh.2015.01.002.

Owens Jr, R. E. (2016). *Language development: An introduction* (9th edn). Instructor.

Paatsch, L., & Nolan, A. (2020). Supporting oral language learning in young children. In A. Kilderry & B. Raban (Eds.), *Strong foundations: evidence informing practice in early childhood education and care* (pp. 156–169). ACER Press. doi:10.37517/978-1-74286-555-3_11.

Paatsch, L., & Toe, D. (2020). The interplay between pragmatics and reading comprehension in children who are deaf or hard of hearing. In *The Oxford handbook of deaf studies in literacy* (pp. 157–170). doi:10.1093/oxfordhb/9780197508268.013.12.

Paul, R. (2007). *Language disorders from infancy through adolescence: Assessment & intervention* (Vol. 324). Elsevier Health Sciences.

Quinn, S., Donnelly, S., & Kidd, E. (2018). The relationship between symbolic play and language acquisition: A meta-analytic review. *Developmental review*, 49, 121–135. doi:10.1016/j.dr.2018.05.005.

Reynolds, E., Stagnitti, K., & Kidd, E. (2011). Play, language and social skills of children attending a play-based curriculum school and a traditionally structured classroom curriculum school in low socioeconomic areas. *Australasian Journal of Early Childhood*, 36(4), 120–130. doi:10.1177/183693911103600416.

Schmid, H. J., & Schmid, H. J. (Eds.) (2012). *Cognitive pragmatics* (Vol. 1). De Gruyter Mouton.

Stagnitti, K. (2004). Understanding play: Implications for play assessment. *Australian Occupational Therapy Journal*, 51, 3–12.

Stagnitti, K., Bailey, A., Hudspeth Stevenson, E., Reynolds, E., & Kidd, E. (2016). An investigation into the effect of play-based instruction on the development of play skills and oral language. *Journal of Early Childhood Research*, 14(4), 389–406. doi:10.1177/1476718X15579741.

Stagnitti, K., & Lewis, F. M. (2015). Quality of pre-school children's pretend play and subsequent development of semantic organization and narrative re-telling skills. *International Journal of Speech-Language Pathology*, 17(2), 148–158. doi:10.3109/17549507.2014.941934.

Stagnitti, K. E., Paatsch, L., Nolan, A., & Campbell, K. (2020). Identifying play skills that predict children's language in the beginning of the first year of school. *Early Years*, 1–15. doi:10.1080/09575146.2020.1865280.

Vygotsky, L. S. (1967). Play and its role in the mental development of the child. *Soviet Psychology*, 5(3), 6–18. doi:10.2753/RPO1061-040505036

Vygotsky, L. S. (1978). *Mind in society: The development of higher mental processes*. Harvard University Press.

Zigler, E. F., Singer, D. G., & Bishop-Josef, S. J. (2004). *Children's play: The roots of reading*. Zero To Three/National Center for Infants, Toddlers and Families.

Zosh, J. M., Gaudreau, C., Golinkoff, R. M., & Hirsh-Pasek, K. (2022). The power of playful learning in the early childhood setting. *Young Children*, 77(2), 6–13. Retrieved from http://ezproxy.deakin.edu.au/login?url=https://www.proquest.com/scholarly-journals/power-playful-learning-early-childhood-setting/docview/2680629720/se-2.

4 Emotional Understanding, Self-Regulation, and Play

To understand emotion is a relatively complex yet integral developmental capacity. Engaging with our surrounding environment, be that the social or the physical environment, requires the ability to navigate conscious- and below the level of conscious understanding of emotions. Emotion and emotional understanding provide a framework for meaningful connections because we can then interpret and predict emotions in others. Rooted deeply within layers of our biology, autobiographical story or back story, and behaviour, emotional understanding is a uniquely developing process, dependent on the interactions of the individual with those around them, and the individual's developing neurobiology (Brown, 2021). As noted in previous chapters, brain development occurs in a hierarchical manner, with a sense of safety being fundamental. Therefore, through kind, nurturing, and patient interactions with others, children will seek out further interactions resulting in strong emotional understanding and positive, joyful connections.

At birth, children are vulnerable, reliant on those around them to not only meet their survival needs but support integration of developing emotional needs as well (Siegel, 2020; Siegel & Bryson, 2011; Sunderland, 2007). As children grow and develop, they experience strong emotions. These strong emotions can be overwhelming, potentially scary, and difficult to understand for the developing child and at times the carers around them (Sunderland, 2007). Here children could be described as being hijacked by strong emotions. During these times children need co-regulated support from a healthy caring adult. It is in the interactions with others that children's most basic understandings of emotion begin to emerge (Siegel, 2020).

Through the narrative of their daily lives, children are immersed in daily experiences, and begin to make connections between what they might be feeling and what it is that is happening. These interactions are important. They form the process through which children develop the capacity for self-regulation, integration (being emotion and language coming together) and an awareness of the world around them. Dan Siegel (2020), a clinical professor of psychiatry, writes in a very meaningful and accessible way, about the importance of understanding the developing self within the collective of others. His work, highly translatable, emphasises how the understanding of interpersonal interactions translates across to our understanding of emotion, therefore creating a platform for meaningful

DOI: 10.4324/9781003296782-5

connection. Meaningful connections develop on the premise that a child is developing the capacity for emotional understanding and self-regulation.

What is self-regulation?

An important capacity in the development of emotional understanding is self-regulation. Self-regulation is not easily defined nor is it operationalised at present to allow us to measure a child's developing capacity. A theoretical definition is presented here that attempts to define the complex nature of self-regulation as

> Whilst engaging in daily activities, individuals are concurrently *monitoring* and *acting* on the integration of cognitive processes and emotion to achieve a goal, and attempting to *manage* internal states of emotion whilst *monitoring* the external expression of behaviour to achieve a sense of belonging.
>
> (Casey, 2017, p. 118)

We will now unpack this definition and discuss the meaning behind its components, identifying what these components might look like when observing children in interactions with others.

"Engaging in daily activities" includes all the activities a child might need, want, or is required to do. This will include a range of play, self-care, social-emotional interactions, receiving direct instructions, a sense of being (whether solitary or in a collective space), and academic pursuits. Whilst engaging in such activities, children are at times consciously attributing to the processes relayed from the cerebellum (an older part of the brain that is at the base of the brain), subconsciously monitoring (receiving and processing information) about their interactions not only with the physical space but the social interactions that exist around their participation. Whilst monitoring themselves and others, children are drawing on cognitive processes. Depending on age, this might include accessing previous learnings, working towards the capacity to plan, forward think, hypothesise, and focus attention.

Previous interactions with their caregivers and significant others may have supported children to connect language and emotion, so here children are starting to connect the "how they feel" with "their actions". This is a complex and evolving process that continues throughout the life course; however, we must not underestimate how capable children are of understanding more complex emotional processes if given the opportunity (Sunderland, 2007). Actions begin to emerge, and those actions either match or mismatch the situation. This is where the ability to manage internal states of emotion emerges and children's capacity for theory of mind is challenged. Theory of mind will be discussed in the following section. Depending on a child's understanding of emotion and the emotions of others, they can then monitor their external expression (for example, their actions in response to an interaction) to achieve a sense of belonging. Complex though this is, this process can happen quite naturally in an environment where the child receives love, care, and nurturance, whatever their underlying biology, biography, behaviour, and back story.

Theory of mind

Theory of mind is recognised as the ability to read complex social situations by understanding a wide range of mental states, such as perception, intention, cognition, biases, and emotion (Baron-Cohen, 1996; Hughes & Leekam, 2004). It is a capacity that supports an individual's understanding that others can have different beliefs or thoughts to oneself about the same scenario, or in the case of play, the same objects and actions (Baron-Cohen, 1996; Hughes & Leekam, 2004). For example, a box may be represented as a car in the story of racing up the mountain. A play partner in the play scenario might suggest it is an aeroplane instead. This is a simplified example of how two children come together and begin to understand that they can think differently about the same object. From here, often a level of negotiation follows as the children strive to gain a playful connection and shared meaning in their play. Depending on their capacity for self-regulation and emotional understanding they will manage their internal states, monitor their external expression and act to either continue the play narrative or alternatively, the play connection will break down.

The development of emotional understanding through play

Theory of mind is believed to be heralded by the onset of pretend play, with pretending being one of the first mental states in development (Baron-Cohen, 1996). As children come together with a play partner, as early as 12 months of age, they begin to consider a single action of pretend. This single action is repeated, for example pretending to drink from a cup or pretending to sleep. Here infants are developing an awareness of a purposeful pretend action (Stagnitti, 2021). If this happens within a social play space of another, such as primary caregivers in the early stages, their play thinking is advanced by the interaction with a caring adult (Stagnitti, 2021). For example, a child may begin to put two actions together, attributes might be given to those actions, such as "yummy", or "snoring" when pretending to sleep. The child's play partner can imitate the child or join in on the play. Here children are developing a skill of joint attention as the child and adult play. In the example of having a cup of tea, the cup is the object at the centre of the play, and it is eye gaze, focussed attention, and joyful connection with another around the cup that is considered joint attention.

Joint attention is the beginning stage of what is identified as developing shared attention. When sharing a play space with another by the age of 2 years, children begin to understand the intentionality of the play; for example, we are pretending to drink with teddy when we have a teapot, teddy, cups, and spoon (Rakoczy, 2008; Stagnitti, 2021). We can come together with these objects, and we can play tea parties. Teddy begins to be represented as "alive", and we include talking to teddy in the play.

Emotions are explored both implicitly and explicitly, and the cerebellum is working below our level of consciousness to develop internal models, or patterns, to help the child to respond to social interactions moment to moment, to perceive verbal and non-verbal cues for understanding emotion and therefore how to respond instantaneously within shared play (Van Overwalle et al., 2020). From here, this shared capacity continues to develop in the play space with others. By 3.5 years of age children are starting to explore the rules of play: what are these objects, how are the objects used, where are we playing, and is the play story changing? Associative social play around 3.5 years of age is very chatty. There is lots of talking about what the children are doing in their play; however, they are yet to create a narrative together (Stagnitti, 2021). They are aware that other children might be using certain types of objects in their play, and a sense of awareness is developing of not acquiring those objects by force. In Australian Aboriginal culture, however, no-one owns the toys, so children mix and match toys fluently with other children (Dender & Stagnitti, 2017). Children's tolerances of being in a play space with others is challenged and the capacity for a developing window of tolerance is supported.

Children are working towards maintaining a shared understanding of the play narrative from 4 years of age, whilst developing skills around self-regulation, and with the capacity of social competence. As children develop in their complexity in play so does the capacity for theory of mind. Children begin to understand more complex mental states such as bias, bluffing, moral dilemmas, the ambiguity of truths, beliefs about beliefs (Hughes & Leekam, 2004). This deeper under-standing of the mental state of others can be observed as children move into more complex play scenarios that span the space of hours, with play stories that continue over days and weeks. At this complex level of play children are negotiating, cooperating, monitoring their own boundaries, and establishing emotional understanding through theory of mind capacity. Rakoczy's (2008) work supports this concept that play is more than children coming together and combining actions. He argues for moments of collective ("we" intentionality) intentions that cannot be simply reduced to, for instance, the combining of two individual intentions in the play (Rakoczy, 2008). Rakoczy's work suggests that the earliest development of social and emotional capacities in pretend play is stronger than previously thought.

Components of self-regulation

Siegel (2012) provides a conceptual understanding for key skills involved in the development of self-regulation. Casey (2017) utilised this concept to observe and understand how self-regulation developed over time during the transition from preschool to formal schooling. Casey analysed children's observed school beha-viour using Siegel's (2012) work alongside Susan Harter's (2012) construction of the self theory, and provided an interpretation for how these concepts might be applied within the context of the early years at school. Below are seven key com-ponents that make up the capacity for self-regulation. These components allow for a closer observation of how a child might be interacting within the social play space with others.

The seven key skills are defined as follows:

- Intensity: The intensity of emotions is monitored by the brain. Daily experiences throughout early childhood influence the intensity of emotions experienced by the child. Depending on the caregiver's response in the early years to moments of children being hijacked (that is, unexpected, unplanned, and unforeseen experiences), the subsequent intensity of expression in interactions with others can either match or mismatch the situation. For example, the child will monitor the level of intensity they need to bring to a play space with others and this will result in a right fit for play or not. If, however, they have *not* found themselves in a supportive co-regulated space with peers or adults, children may misread the level of intensity they need to bring to a scenario. Children's higher than needed level of emotional intensity, if responded to in a supportive way by peers or adults, provides an opportunity for children to continue to develop self-regulatory skills.
- Sensitivity: Sensitivity can be determined by a person's response to any given daily experience. It involves the amount of stimulus that elicits a response, leading to potential flexibility or inflexibility. Over- versus under-sensitivity can be related to the developing neurobiology of the child. For example, a younger child will often be oversensitive and a tantrum may ensue. Co-regulation with another will support children's developing sensitivity to daily experiences. Children will then respond to the environment, interpreting it either as a state of safety (where they will begin to calm down) or a stressed state of fear or anxiety (where their emotions will heighten or shut down) (Dana, 2018).
- Specificity: Specificity involves giving meaning and value to daily experiences. A child's engagement in daily experiences creates meaning, allowing for the opportunity to monitor and activate the integration of cognitive processes and emotion. Childhood development of specificity begins at pleasure/discomfort in infancy. Over time, pleasure develops to surprise, interest, and joy (Harter, 2012). Discomfort develops towards fear, anger, and weariness, frustration/ distress, disgust, and shame (Harter, 2012). Specificity is potentially a result of emotion centres in the right side of the brain integrating with language acquisition around those emotions, on the left side (see also Chapter 2). This integration can be supported most efficiently in a guided play scenario, with adults providing the scaffolding around interpretations of emotions experienced and language attributed to those.
- Windows of tolerance: Thinking or behaviour can become disrupted if arousal moves beyond the boundaries of a child's window of tolerance. A window of tolerance refers to a child's tolerance level for coping with internal and external emotions. A child's window of tolerance may be narrow or wide, dependant on previous daily experiences with caregivers. Temperament and conditions such as hunger and tiredness also influence the window of tolerance, which is usually observed as a reduction in the tolerance level. When children move outside the window of tolerance a lower mode of processing is

likely to take place (Siegel, 2012). This results in a reduction in children's capacity to draw on previous learning, to access the conscious, and potentially problem-solve, plan ahead, and think. Children throughout the early years will often move outside of their window of tolerance, and it is the supportive interactions with others that will support the development of widening their window.

- Recovery processes: Recovery processes are the ability of the child to reflect on the mental state of oneself and of others (theory of mind capacity) and to understand more deeply their own and other's emotions. This theory of mind capacity is beginning to emerge in the 5–7-year age range (Hughes & Leekam, 2004). This process involves children moving back within the window of tolerance because of the ability for self-initiated self-reflection and impulse control. In the early years, primarily up to the age of 8 years, children will continue to benefit from support to recover and make sense of the narrative around why they moved outside of their window of tolerance.

- Access to consciousness: Siegel (2012) suggests the self is created by non-conscious processes and the selective associations of those processes into the conscious. Children aged 5–7 years are beginning to develop the ability for metacognition. They are aware of others' thoughts and perceptions; however, they are unable to consider those thoughts and perceptions in reflection to themselves (Harter, 1996; 2012). That is, children cannot yet evaluate whether what other people say about them is true for them. Here access to consciousness is considered in terms of the child's awareness of others and themselves in creating meaningful interactions. Awareness of self and others is supported through guided play interactions with others. Children need to experience moment-to-moment interactions and connections to begin to develop an awareness of self and others.

- External expression: Rules exist amongst cultures for behaviour that might be considered appropriate/inappropriate to the public eye. This capacity is beginning to develop around the age of 5 years as children become more aware of the thoughts and perceptions of others and what is appropriate within their culture (Harter, 2012). As children develop this emotional self-regulation, there will be times when differences exist between the display of behaviour that represents a child's inner core feelings as opposed to their adaptive self. External expression then provides an opportunity for a feedback loop; for example, if children are expressing themselves in a playful manner within play, then others will join them. If there is a sense of rigidity and inflexibility in their play interactions, then others will move away.

There are developmental steps involved in play interactions with others that support the opportunity for children to explore and develop each of these seven key skills of self-regulation. With reference to the Learn to Play Framework (Stagnitti, 2021, also see Chapter 10 for the Pretend Play Checklist for Teachers), each developmental milestone in pretend play across the six key skills (i.e., play scripts, sequences of play actions, object substitution, doll/teddy play, role play, and social development) is linked to opportunities to build more complex levels of emotional understanding and self-regulation alongside language development. Children who have not had the opportunity to build more complex play skills have a reduced opportunity to explore the seven key self-regulatory skills.

Patterns of change in self-regulation development

Casey (2017) in her longitudinal 3-year study "Resilience in Early Years: Understanding Pretend Play and Self-Regulation Development" identified patterns of development for pretend play and self-regulation for a cohort of children considered resilient by their preschool teacher. The study observed changes in play and interpersonal interactions within a classroom setting across a transition from preschool through to the second year of formal schooling. The 3-year longitudinal study clearly identified patterns of play and self-regulation development. Most noteworthy was the experience of those children who continued to develop pretend play skills above the ability expected for their age. Observations identified that their interactions within the classroom environment demonstrated opportunity to explore all seven key skills of self-regulation. Those children whose play skills remained below the expected range for age experienced fewer opportunities for social interaction, and therefore stayed within the space of exploring their window of tolerance and recovery process, which is considered less advanced exploration for their respective age.

Interestingly within this study, out of the 24 children identified as resilient by their preschool teacher, 15 developed pretend play skills above the expected range for age by Year 1 (second year of formal schooling). The pretend play skills were measured using a norm referenced standardised play assessment, the Child Initiated Pretend Play Assessment (ChIPPA) (Stagnitti, 2022). Play assessments were administered by occupational therapists who were unaware of the child's developmental profile. The advancement in play skills then led to the opportunity for more integrated and complex ways of interacting and engaging with their peers. Over time, the study identified, through a grounded theory approach, that children

> prioritise the value and meaning ascribed to their daily activities. Cognitive processes are utilised concurrently with intensity and attention to understand the relationship between the self and the environment. External expression is consolidating as self-representation develops. Regulation according to context was conscious rather than intuitive.
>
> (Casey, 2017, p. 160)

There were developmental milestones across the three years of the study that identified children's capacity as being greater than the initial definition of self-regulation given at the beginning of this chapter. The initial definition suggested self-regulation was occurring intuitively, below the level of conscious monitoring. As play skills developed to a more complex level, a more advanced level of thinking occurred. Children were consciously exploring their self-representation within the social context of others. This is indicative of a more advanced capacity for self-regulation and consequently emotional understanding. Figure 4.1 is a visual representation depicting the relationship between more complex pretend play skills and opportunity for self-regulation development.

Bodrova et al. (2013) outline the work of Daniel Elkonin, a student of Lev Vygotsky. Elkonin (1978, as cited in Bodrova et al., 2013), described the link between what he described as a mature form of play and self-regulatory ability theory. Bodrova et al. (2013) argued for studies such as the study outlined above to explore the link between pretend play ability and the broader classroom observations focused on self-regulation, and the dynamic relationship between play and self-regulation. Research is almost at the point of establishing a causal connection between pretend play and self-regulation development. The resultant outcomes for children are a greater level of emotional understanding, a wider opportunity to explore self-representation, more advanced levels of language acquisition, and a greater awareness of mental states. Interestingly, Lev Vygotsky (1967, p. 14) identified the self-regulatory demands that are placed upon a child when engaging in a social peer play space:

> At every step the child is faced with a conflict between the rule of the game and what he would do if he could suddenly act spontaneously. In the game he acts counter to what he wants … [achieving] the maximum display of willpower.

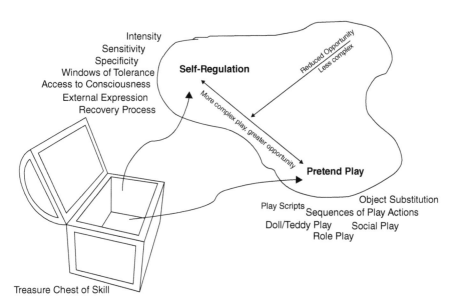

Figure 4.1 A visual representation of the relationship between more complex pretend play skills and self-regulation development

Why is this important?

Whilst engaging socially with peers or a competent adult (in an adult-supported rather than adult-directed condition) children are also developing skills in emotional intelligence, through exploring the ability to understand their own internal thoughts and those of others (Sunderland, 2007). Berk et al. (2006) found that when children participated in make-believe play with a supportive adult, greater improvement in self-regulatory abilities such as modulation of speed of behaviour, inhibition of impulse, and planning were highlighted in contrast to children who participated in adult-directed scenarios. In a study on the role of sociodramatic play in supporting self-regulation, Elias and Berk (2002) found that complex sociodramatic play (also called social pretend play) improved the capacity for self-regulation in children, who were identified as highly impulsive, with self-regulation measured at circle time and clean-up time.

Throughout Siobhan's time working in the field in several kindergarten/childcare and school settings, Siobhan has met very energetic and equally exasperated educators along the way. The following discussion is extremely pertinent to current times. Many children are entering the education setting with less complex pretend play ability (Reynolds et al., 2011; Stagnitti et al., 2020). The resultant challenges that arise are children who come to school with difficulty in modulating their behaviour, potentially a feeling of dysregulation, and reduced capacity to explore seven of the key self-regulation skills. This can also be observed in children's reduced opportunity to engage with peers. Challenges then arise in the children's ability to focus and attend to task, reducing their ability to understand and create narrative, and therefore they miss key components of the classroom discourse and the ability to engage in learning.

As many educators are managing these challenges with children's behaviour, there tends to be a shift towards direct instruction. Children will learn from direct instruction; however, the learning outcomes for children are best supported through a guided approach (Zosh et al., 2017; 2018). A guided approach will support children to actively explore, expand their curiosity and seek out further learning opportunities (Weisberg et al., 2015). Therefore, children's opportunities to engage in guided play in the early years are crucial, not only for the impact on individual development, but also for interconnectedness that suggests people do not operate in isolation. Interactions are always influenced by the collective, and there is an interplay between educator and student engagement. The guided approach to learning, particularly within a play-based learning environment, provides greater opportunity for self-regulation, emotional understanding, moment to moment responses in interactions with others, and ultimately satisfaction for both educator and student.

Application of knowledge for learning through play

Several scenarios come to mind when describing how play might support self-regulation and emotional understanding in the classroom environment. Below is an example of one significant moment that gave a group of children a sense of joy from connecting with others in play. From the beginning, Siobhan Casey's role within the school was to assess all foundation children's play skills before entering the first year of formal learning in primary school. This process involved assessing the children's play ability across Term 1 using both the ChIPPA and the Pretend Play Checklist for Teachers (PPCT). Alongside the children's transition statements and educator observations, Siobhan and the teachers were able to gain an extensive developmental profile for the children, identifying their strengths and areas of support needed. Siobhan was able to gain a deep understanding of the child's developmental play, and was therefore able to group children according to their play strengths.

Within the school Siobhan provided guided support to teachers in running developmental play sessions for the whole class. These sessions were designed to support children's developing self-initiated pretend play skills. Informed by play assessment, children were grouped in play scenarios dependant on their developmental level of play. Here is an example of one group of children, four males, who came together to play around a car mat. The car mat can be described as a floor mat which has roads, a hospital and supermarket, a park, and a school. Children with a developmental play understanding around the age of 3–3.5 years begin to understand the wider context of the car mat scenarios and develop narrative around this play object. Independently, the four boys had strengths in their play that suggested they would cope with this scenario and potentially create a short narrative consisting of four to five play actions in a sequence.

The play scenario began in a child-directive context; they were presented with the car mat, some vehicles and off to the side of the mat, animals, blocks, and characters were available. These play materials were enough to support the development of a story, but not too much as to be overwhelming. Siobhan described what was available to the boys and encouraged them to play what they wanted. They were keen and highly motivated to start playing. Siobhan did not direct the play and allowed the boys to initiate their own ideas. This also created an environment where the boys felt safe to bring their ideas to the play scenario.

The play began with the four boys enthusiastically driving their cars around the mat, at times crashing into one another, climbing over one another, with windows of tolerance being tested. There were four children playing out their own independent actions that consisted of one pretend action, that is, driving a car. This represented a less complex form of play. Opportunities to connect with others were reduced, there was very little awareness of others, reduced opportunity for language acquisition, no reciprocal dialogue or actions occurring, windows of tolerance were being tested, without the opportunity to explore the seven key skills of self-regulation. The boys presented almost in a state of competition rather than connection, and as a result, adrenaline was starting to kick in and cortisol levels were rising. This was not a joyful play space, it was very challenging, and in a free play scenario, one or more of the boys would have walked away to play somewhere else.

In a guided play scenario, Siobhan was able to scaffold the play to work towards the establishment of a shared narrative and greater awareness of others in the car mat play. Drawing on the understanding of the Learn to Play Framework and the underlying principles that guide practice to engage children to build their play capacity, Siobhan modelled the pretend action of driving the car. Siobhan did this in a way that explicitly highlighted an awareness of her body and others in space through the play. For example, Siobhan would drive the car saying "Beep, Beep I am just behind you", or "Beep, Beep, I am turning this way", or "Beep, Beep, I am heading to the supermarket". As Siobhan did this, she would demonstrate to the boys how she would move her body around the outside of the car mat, demonstrating awareness of others in the play space and being mindful of her own actions in the play. This worked!

With encouragement and some brief reminders in a positive supportive manner, the boys were able to create some repetition of the one pretend action of driving cars around the car mat. As they did this in response to the modelling of how to drive their cars, the boys played with an increased awareness of those around them. It was joyful play. Then the boys subsequently began to calm down. At the point at which Siobhan felt they had calmed down and were ready to extend the play, she added some animals and characters to the vehicle. The play narrative had begun. The boys would visit the animals either patting them or bringing them some food. From this point in the play, two boys worked together to build a veterinary clinic. This involved meta play, metacommunication skills, very basic levels of negotiation and cooperation. The animals would come to the vet when they were sick. Siobhan's role here became to encourage the boys to engage within a short narrative of four to five different, sequential play actions, create some consistency to their story, and continue to provide some supportive prompts around awareness of themselves and others in the play. The play was stopped only by the bell indicating break time. This was followed by all the boys asking, "can we do that again?" Siobhan walked away with a deep sense of satisfaction. Siobhan had also coached the teacher through the play action. Discussion with the teacher followed, Siobhan explaining how this play supported the development of the boys but also how this play could be connected to the curriculum. Siobhan understood what that play moment meant to the boys and how deeply supportive it was of their developing self-regulation and emotional understanding.

Conclusion

Research has explored the link between pretend play, self-regulation, and subsequent emotional understanding. Greater complexity in children's pretend play provides greater opportunity to develop seven key capacities involved in self-regulation development. As children engage in a collective play space with peers, they work to negotiate storylines and they explore the emotion of the narrative, through reciprocal dialogue and actions. Reading non-verbal cues and drawing on internal models of understanding, children explore emotional understanding. Guided play opportunities foster teacher involvement in supporting children to regulate their interactions with others by providing an awareness of the seven key capacities of self-regulation through playful language and scaffolding. Teachers provide language around the development of emotion and emotional understanding by playing in a guided, shared manner implicitly, and sometimes explicitly, by modelling the rules around emotion, emotional understanding of others, and self-regulation.

References

Baron-Cohen, S. (1996). *Mindblindness: An essay on autism and theory of mind*. MIT Press.

Berk, L. E., Mann, T. D., & Ogan, A. T. (2006). Make-believe play: Wellspring for development of self-regulation. In D. G. Singer, R. M. Gollinkoff & K. Hirsh-Pasek (Eds.), *Play=learning: How play motivates and enhances children's cognitive and social emotional growth* (pp. 74–100). Oxford University Press.

Bodrova, E., Germeroth, C., & Leong, D. (2013). Play and self-regulation: Lessons from Vygotsky. *American Journal of Play*, 6, 111–123.

Brown, B. (2021). *Atlas of heart: Mapping meaningful connection and the language of human experience*. Penguin House.

Casey, S. (2017). Resilience in early years: Understanding pretend play and self-regulation development. Unpublished doctoral thesis. Deakin University, Geelong, Australia.

Dana, D. (2018). *The polyvagal theory in therapy: Engaging the rhythm of regulation*. W. W. Norton.

Dender, A., & Stagnitti, K. (2017). Content and cultural validity in the development of the Indigenous Play Partner Scale. *Australian Occupational Therapy Journal*, 64, 283–293. doi:10.1111/1440-1630.12355.

Elias, C. L., & Berk, L. E. (2002). Self-regulation in young children: is there a role for sociodramatic play? *Early Childhood Research Quarterly*, 17(2), 216–238. doi:10.1016/S0885-2006(02)00146-1.

Harter, S. (1996). Developmental changes in self-understanding across the 5 to 7 shift. In A. Sameroff & M. M. Haith (Eds.), *The five to seven year shift: The age of reason and responsibility*. University of Chicago Press.

Harter, S. (2012). *The construction of the self: Developmental and sociocultural foundations*. Guilford Press.

Hughes, C., & Leekam, S. (2004). What are the links between theory of mind and social relations? Review, reflections and new directions for studies of typical and atypical development. *Social Development*, 13, 590–619. doi:10.1111/j.1467-9507.2004.00285.x.

Rakoczy, H. (2008). Pretence as individual and collective intentionality. *Mind and Language*, 23(5), 499–517. doi:10.1111/j.1468–0017.2008.00357.x.

Reynolds, E., Stagnitti, K., & Kidd, E. (2011). Play, language and social skills of children attending a play-based curriculum school and a traditionally structured classroom curriculum school in low socioeconomic areas. *Australasian Journal of Early Childhood*, 4, 120. doi:10.1177/183693911103600416.

Siegel, D. J. (2012). *The developing mind: How relationships and the brain interact to shape who we are* (2nd edn). Guilford Press.

Siegel, D. J. (2020). *The developing mind: How relationships and the brain interact to shape who we are* (3rd edn). Guilford Press.

Siegel, D. J., & Bryson, T.P. (2011). *The whole-brain child: Twelve revolutionary strategies to nurture your child's developing mind*. Tarcher.

Stagnitti, K. (2022). *Child-initiated pretend play assessment* (2nd edn). Learn to Play. www.learntoplayevents.com.

Stagnitti, K. (2021). *Learn to Play Therapy: Principles, processes and practical activities.* Learn to Play. www.learntoplayevents.com.

Stagnitti, K. E., Paatsch, L., Nolan, A.,, & Campbell, K. (2020). Identifying play skills that predict children's language in the beginning of the first year of school. *Early Years*, 1–15. doi:10.1080/09575146.2020.1865280.

Sunderland, M. (2007). *What every parent needs to know: The remarkable effects of love, nurture and play on your child's development.* Dorling Kindersley.

Van Overwalle, F., Manto, M., Cattaneo, Z., Clausi, S., Ferrari, C., Gabrieli, J., Guell, X., Helven, E., Lupo, M., Va, Q., Michelutti, M., Olivito, G., Pu, M., Rice, L., Schmahmann, J., Siciliano, L., Sokolov, A., Stoodley, C., van Dun, K., … Leggio, M. (2020). Consensus paper: Cerebellum and social cognition. *Cerebellum*, 19, 833–868. doi:10.1007/s12311-020-01155-1.

Vygotsky, Lev S. (1967). Play and its role in the mental development of the child. *Soviet Psychology*, 5, 6–18.

Weisberg, D. S., Kittredge, A. K., Hirsh-Pasek, K., Golinkoff, R. M., & Klahr, D. (2015). Making play work for education. *Phi Delta Kappan*, 96(8), 8–13. doi:10.1177/0031721715583955.

Zosh, J., Hirsh-Pasek, K., Hopkins, E., Jensen, H., Liu, C., Neale, D., Solis, L., & Whitebread, D. (2018). Assessing the inaccessible: Redefining play as a spectrum. *Frontiers in Psychology*, 9, 1–12. doi:10.3389/fpsyg.2018.01124.

Zosh, J. M., Hopkins, E. J., Jensen, H., Liu, C., Neale, D., Hirsh-Pasek, K., Solis, S. L., & Whitebread, D. (2017). *Learning through play: A review of the evidence.* White paper. LEGO Foundation. https://cms.learningthroughplay.com/media/wmtlmbe0/learning-through-play_web.pdf.

5 Developing Personal Social Capabilities Through Play

Children are social beings. Making friends and playing are part of a rich childhood, and personal social capabilities are integral to the ability to play with others. The term "personal social capabilities" is defined in this chapter as "being able to interact with others in the moment, with understanding of the meaning, in verbal and non-verbal social interactions, including understanding the intention of others". Not only is it "an important foundation for school readiness" (Bruder & Chen, 2007, p. 49), but the more socially engaged we are, regardless of age, the higher our level of cognitive performance (Ybarra et al., 2008). In essence, if we desire to nurture a classroom where children can work together, make friends, and perform complex cognitive tasks to the best of their abilities, then a knowledge of how to develop personal social capabilities is a welcome addition to our skill set.

Aspects of personal social capabilities explored in this chapter are: theory of mind, cognition, and verbal and non-verbal aspects of social interaction, including metacommunication. Research relating to personal social capabilities and pretend play is then explored, along with opportunities for learning and development during child–teacher interactions. The chapter concludes by applying knowledge of personal social capabilities to learning through play, with a section on "Learning from Experience". A time limited play program that assisted a classroom of five- to six-year-old children to develop social capabilities through pretend play skill building is explained.

What are personal social capabilities?

Personal social capabilities are a person's ability to engage with others socially, so that shared meaning in the interaction is created, which in turn, allows the interaction to be sustained. Personal social capabilities are akin to social competence and being socially interactive, reflecting a child's ability to understand behavioural, cognitive, and affective interactions and adapt to varied social environments (McAloney & Stagnitti, 2009, p. 99). In pretend play environments, the highest complexity of skills is within complex pretend play, when children are engaged in cooperative play and can sustain "reciprocal dialogue and reciprocal action between peers" (Whitebread & O'Sullivan, 2012, p. 200). The socio-constructivist perspective regards social experiences as influential in a child's

DOI: 10.4324/9781003296782-6

development and capacity building, with play itself being a context for further development, as well as interaction with capable peers and adults (Nicolopoulou et al., 2010; Vygotsky, 2016; Whitebread & O'Sullivan, 2012).

Personal social capabilities include non-verbal communication and embodiment, such as understanding a person's non-verbal gestures and actions, their facial expressions, vocal tones, body and hand gestures. In complex social interactions, understanding both the literal meaning of the words, as well as an appreciation for the underlying meaning of what was said, is necessary. In order to fully understand the meaning of verbal interactions, you must also understand the non-verbal information, conveyed through the speaker's facial expression, body movement or posture, and tone of voice. This understanding also incorporates understandings of how language is used in social contexts (pragmatics) (Wang et al., 2006; also see Chapter 3 for a deeper discussion of pragmatics).

Equally essential to fully understanding social interactions is the skill of understanding mental states, also known as "theory of mind" (Hughes & Leekam, 2004; Zosh et al., 2017). Theory of mind involves "reading" the intention or motivation of others (Hughes & Leekam, 2004). For example, "Is the person I am socially interacting with; genuine, joking, bored, interested or bluffing?" Hughes and Leekam (2004) advise that theory of mind understanding can have positive, neutral, or negative impacts on a child's social interactions. For example, a positive outcome might be empathy, whereas a negative outcome could be increased sensitivity to criticism (Hughes & Leekam, 2004, p. 607). Meta-communication, discussed further in this chapter, can support children's learning to enhance positive outcomes and reduce the impact of negative outcomes.

For development of theory of mind to occur, and for social interactions to be sustained and adjusted in the moment, exposure to a variety of social interactions is needed, such as:

- conversations about how the child is feeling and what they are thinking,
- shared pretend play,
- narratives,
- exposure to, and conversations about, deception (Hughes & Leekam, 2004).

When children understand the meaning of the interaction, can sustain social interactions with others, and can adjust their interactions in moment-by-moment social exchanges, they are seen as having personal social capabilities.

Why is this important?

"Social competence is an important foundation for school readiness" (Bruder & Chen, 2007, p. 49). It promotes collaborative learning and is one of the five characteristics involved in learning through play (Zosh et al., 2017; 2018; see also Chapter 2). Zosh et al. (2017; 2018) explain that multiple networks in the brain are stimulated through play, particularly those relating to detecting the mental states of others (theory of mind). Understanding the mental states of others is included in "reading" a social situation, and understanding interactions such as bluffing, when bias influences beliefs, moral dilemmas, and perceptions of what a person might be thinking or feeling (Hughes & Leekam, 2004). This ability is critical for teaching and learning interactions. Children communicate both verbally and non-verbally with adults and peers, and without an understanding of how to read social situations, a child's capacity to understand, and be understood by others, is greatly diminished (Zosh et al., 2017).

Collaborative learning, which is when students work together in small groups towards a common learning goal (Gokhale, 1995), requires children to understand mental states as they communicate socially with each other. When children work in small groups towards a common learning goal, the active exchange of ideas promotes critical thinking (Gokhale, 1995). Critical thinking is a cognitive process, and social interactions engage a variety of cognitive processes (Ybarra et al., 2008).

The cognitive processes in a simple social interaction of the exchange of views between two people requires: working memory, paying attention to what is said, adapting to each other's perspectives, inference of beliefs (theory of mind) and inhibiting inappropriate behaviour (Ybarra et al., 2008). Social interaction between children requires children to regulate themselves in response to others so they can maintain the social interaction (Whitebread & O'Sullivan, 2012). When children are socially interactive, they become more flexible, less rigid, and regulate themselves within social interactions (Zosh et al., 2017).

Social engagement and cognitive performance

Examining data from interviews of 3,610 people aged 24–96 years from the *Survey of Americans' Changing Lives*, Ybarra et al. (2008) found that, across all ages, the more socially engaged people were, the higher their level of cognitive performance. In a second study, Ybarra et al. randomly assigned 76 participants aged 18–21 years to one of three conditions. One condition was a social interaction, which involved a discussion for 10 minutes on the pros and cons of privacy protection. Another condition was an intellectual condition, where participants did not interact with each other, and instead spent 10 minutes reading a comprehension task, a crossword puzzle, and a mental rotation task. The control condition was participants, on their own, watching a 10-minute clip from the sitcom *Seinfeld*. Results showed that both the intellectual group and social group outperformed the control group in cognitive tasks. There was no difference between the intellectual group and social group for working memory or speed of processing (Ybarra et al., 2008).

Research on personal social capabilities and pretend play

Personal social capabilities are integral to the ability to play with others. High levels of pretend play and physical play are associated with high emotion understanding, emotion regulation, and emotional competence (see Chapter 4 for more discussion). These qualities translated into improved peer relationships, with boys engaged in more physical play and girls engaged in more pretend play (Lindsay & Colwell, 2003). McAloney and Stagnitti (2009) carried out a study where 53 preschool children aged 4–5 years were assessed using the Child-Initiated Pretend Play Assessment (ChIPPA) and teachers (independently from the researchers) rated the same children using the Penn Interactive Peer Play Scale (PIPPS). They found that children who demonstrated ability in pretend play to create elaborate play scenes, stories, and use objects in substitution were the same children who teachers rated as socially interactive with peers. The socially interactive children were less disruptive and less disconnected from peers (McAloney & Stagnitti, 2009).

Uren and Stagnitti (2009) also carried out a study with 41 children aged 5–7 years using the ChIPPA and the PIPPS. Their findings supported those of McAloney and Stagnitti, with teachers rating socially competent children who were also the children whose pretend play was elaborate, highly organised, and included object substitution. (Object substitution is using objects as symbols in play, for example a box represents a car, or a block represents a phone.) The findings of these studies were consistent with Farmer-Dougan and Kaszuba (1999), who had previously found that the complexity of a child's pretend play was related to the child's social competence.

Uren and Stagnitti (2009) also examined a child's involvement in classroom activities using Leuven's Involvement Scale for Young Children, and found involvement had a significant relationship with social interaction ($r = .43$, $p < .01$) and a child's ability in object substitution ($r = .42$, $p < .01$) and elaborateness of play ($r = .45$, $p < .01$). This suggests that the complexity of a child's pretend play is related to their social competence and involvement in classroom activities.

As children engage with peers in pretend play, they create stories or narratives. It is useful to think of "pretend play and storytelling as falling within the field of narrative activity, on a continuum ranging from the discursive exposition of narratives in storytelling to their enactment in pretend play" (Nicolopoulou et al., 2010, p. 46). In creating stories in play with peers, children create shared meaning of what is happening in the play. They do this through conversational exchanges, which includes extending the ideas of others, introducing a new idea, adding in new props, and showing acceptance or rejection of peers' ideas through verbal and non-verbal communication (Whittington & Floyd, 2009). Chapter 3 provides in-depth analysis of verbal and non-verbal interactions between children.

In an analysis of an adult–child dyad playing together, Wallerstedt et al. (2021, p. 9) concluded that "playing implies constituting a narrative that is enacted and drives the activity". As children play together and create shared meaning in the play, they also understand the intentionality of the play, that is, what the props mean for this play context and the motivations of the characters in the play in this moment (Rakoczy, 2008). Children understand the intentionality of the play as early as 3 years of age. Rakoczy (2008) calls this "collaborative we-intentionality". Understanding the collaborative intentionality of the play also enables children to respond to the play "moment-by-moment", and this occurs from 2 years of age

(Creaghe et al., 2021). Personal social capabilities, then, can be observed when children interact socially and respond moment-by-moment.

Moment-by-moment responses were analysed in an in-depth analysis of an adult and 5-year-old child playing (Wallerstedt et al., 2021). The shifts in the moment-by-moment interactions included clarification of the play ideas, information relating to ideas, reference to the child's own lived experiences, and extension of the narrative (Wallerstedt et al., 2021). The ability to respond moment-by-moment is important for learning when children work in small groups, play with friends, and respond to the social context of the classroom. When children engage in small groups creating stories in pretend play, they are creating narratives, understanding the mental states of others (theory of mind) and socially interacting (Stagnitti, 2021). It is not surprising that socially engaging with others in cooperative, complex pretend play is intellectually demanding (Whitebread & O'Sullivan, 2012).

When children play in pairs or small groups, high levels of collaboration and talk, and metacognitive and self-regulatory behaviours have been observed (Whitebread & O'Sullivan, 2012). Within these play contexts, metacommunication (that is, communication about communication), functions explicitly and implicitly within the play scene.

Explicit metacommunication is both verbal and non-verbal (Whitebread & O'Sullivan, 2012). Explicit metacommunication is used by children to establish which roles the players will undertake in the play, whilst giving context and function to objects within the play scene. Explicit metacommunication sometimes occurs when a child is using a narrator's voice. For example, when directing, or redirecting the play, when settling disputes about what to play, or where the play story might lead next, and when imitating comments from another (de Haan et al., 2021; Whitebread & O'Sullivan, 2012). De Haan et al. (2021) analysed explicit communication comments in the play of 22 children and found explicit metacommunication is used in relation to a higher complexity of the narrative within social pretend play (de Haan et al., 2021).

Implicit metacommunication is within the play scene itself and is least disruptive to the flow of the play because children stay within the play character (Whitebread & O'Sullivan, 2012). With implicit metacommunication, children communicate where the play is going within the play. For example, the child playing a shop keeper may say "I'm closing the shop because I want to go on a holiday". Other child/ren playing may then explicitly discuss their thoughts on where the play should go, as in; "Will we play that you are going on a bus? I could be the driver! I can take you to the zoo!", or implicitly discuss their thoughts "[putting on a hat] Okay, my name is James and I'm your driver today, this bus is stopping at the zoo".

"Metacommunication appears to be a multi-dimensional and multi-functional tool that enables children to express their symbolic thoughts, and to manage their own and their playmates' play behaviour" (de Haan et al., 2021, p. 15 of 19 pp.). In complex play scenarios, children can move seamlessly between explicit and implicit metacommunication, moment-to-moment, throughout the play. Whitebread and O'Sullivan (2012) argue that metacommunication requires metacognition (understanding one's own thinking) and self-regulation as children plan the play together, monitor the play and each other, and negotiate and develop the play. This allows them to maintain and sustain the play with reciprocal interactions that support agreement and create a shared meaning.

Application of knowledge to learning through play

Learning in pairs or small groups, with a common goal, increases a child's critical thinking. It requires thinking and responding to others in the moment, with explicit or implicit metacommunication. Within play, the introduction of object substitution increases verbal interchanges between children as they play and negotiate to establish a shared meaning of the intention of the object in the play (Creaghe et al., 2021). For example, a child might decide that a stick is a magic wand, but until they speak about it, the wand is unlikely to enter the shared storytelling that is social pretend play. When the child speaks about the stick being a magic wand, and the other children accept that the stick is a wand, the meaning becomes shared. The wand then gains the imposed meaning of power to create something magical in the narrative.

Negotiating the meaning of objects in the play involves children conversing with others (Whittington & Floyd, 2009), which involves language. A child's ability in object substitution at ages 4 and 5 years is predictive of a child's oral narrative and language up to four years later (Stagnitti & Lewis, 2015). Object substitution ability has also been found to be a key play skill in predicting a child's expressive and receptive language in their first year of school (Stagnitti et al., 2020). Wallerstedt et al. (2021) have given descriptions of adult–child negotiations when pillows and books were introduced to a play scene as a roof.

Practical ways to include object substitution in a classroom

Teachers can include unstructured objects within small group play to increase children's critical thinking, counterfactual thinking (because you recognise the object, but also hold in your mind that it is a symbol for something else), and metacommunication. You can demonstrate object substitution in a classroom by:

- drawing pictures in a sandpit with a stick and calling the stick your paintbrush,
- using the same stick that you used as a paintbrush to become a wand, transform an object into something more exciting to be imagined whilst reading a story,
- lining ten young children up on a mat, calling it a bed and singing "Ten in the Bed" whilst acting out the song, teaching children to count backwards from 10,
- co-creating a "cubby house" out of bed sheets or curtains to become a "quiet space" for the classroom.

When you pick up any object and demonstrate that it can be something that it is not, you are encouraging counterfactual thinking and problem-solving skills.

Imagining features on an object that aren't there (for example, a plain box for a car with imagined wheels) is higher order thinking. Use metacommunication to demonstrate and encourage pictures to be built in the children's minds and engage them in talking about their own pictures that they imagine in their minds. Through these processes, children learn that there is more than one way to use an object, more than one way to think about things, and more than one possible answer to a question. When you negotiate and talk about thoughts during the process, you increase learning opportunities by using metacommunication to enhance critical thinking.

You may decide to create a "safe space" in your classroom, to assist children who are struggling emotionally (also see Chapter 11). Building the "safe space" with the children can be a co-created learning opportunity, which could build their personal social capabilities, as the design of the "safe space" is negotiated. The design of such a space may require a range of appropriate materials, for example, a bed sheet or oversized cardboard box. The co-creation could begin by the adult saying something like, "Could we use this to create our safe space? I wonder what this could be?" Allowing the children to determine what the materials could become and supporting them to design the space with unstructured objects increases their skills in object substitution, allows for self-initiation of ideas, and negotiation between peers.

Practical ways to increase understanding of character motivations

Stories have characters and reading a story about a character who struggles emotionally, and discussing how challenging that must be for the character, and what that might feel like for the character promotes emotional understanding, theory of mind, and metatalk. A further resource for classroom activities to create characters can be found in Stagnitti and Jellie (2023). A sock puppet could also represent the character (promoting object substitution and theory of mind). You could ask the children to talk to a partner or within a group about what they do when they are struggling with big or difficult feelings, and what might work for the character in the story (explicit metacommunication, encouraging critical thinking).

As children play, they construct a narrative (de Haan et al., 2021; Nicolopoulou et al., 2010). De Haan et al. suggest that teachers can use explicit metacommunication for children whose narrative skills are low. For example, teachers can encourage role play, puppet play, or small world play, where teachers and children explicitly communicate aspects of the play narrative such as the roles of characters and development of the plot, which may enable children to understand character motivation and narrative structure more clearly. Using these techniques in guided play brings social interaction and agency to children, as they are motivated to engage in problem solving within the play.

When children have mastered personal social capabilities, they are able to be split into groups with greater ease and work together. They make friendships; new children are less isolated, integrate, and feel socially connected. Increased social connection reduces friction between children and requires less teacher intervention

(Stagnitti et al., 2013). When children play, they have more opportunities to practise being more flexible and adaptable to changes in the environment, in the moment. For example, if a child or another group of children approach, can they be accommodated into the play, without interrupting the play.

A practical example

At a small school in regional Queensland, Australia, Amity Green prepared six 1-hour play sessions. Using a demonstration of a play skill, as per Stagnitti's *Learn to Play* manual (2021), children were explicitly shown, through playing out a short scene, one of each of the play skills of: play scripts, doll and teddy play, role play, object substitution, and play sequences, for approximately 15–20 minutes before a session. Children were then given semi-structured free play, with access to provided materials and found objects from around their classroom. Amity observed the children and supported their play.

Prior to the first session, the classroom teacher advised Amity that there were several children who struggled to integrate socially in class. Two were described as "bossy" by the other children. Despite appearing strong and independent, one child told Amity that she felt sad and lonely. The other was accepted as a leader in her group, but her play was described by her teacher as being "tolerated" by the other children, and the play was not enjoyable for others. A third child was frequently excluded from games in groups, playing cooking games by himself. His teacher advised that he rarely changed play scripts but appeared to enjoy playing "cooking" alone. This child said that the other children didn't play with him, so that's why he just played cooking games by himself. A fourth child was described as sad and possibly depressed. His play ability was exceptional, but the games he played were not tolerated by more dominant members of the group, so he rarely suggested play ideas. The remainder of the children were divided into small groups of two or four, and played well within their group, but rarely included new players.

In the session, Amity spoke about play scripts, and showed the children how play can be like storytelling. Stories can be about people, what they do at home, things that they do when they go away from home, things that they have done or seen or only heard about, and even things that are completely made up. Sometimes there are problems that need to be solved, and the play can be quick, or it can go for days or weeks.

After assessing the approximate play level of the class, Amity demonstrated a play script at a level most children would comprehend, which was a story about a teddy that needed to go to the doctor, because of a hurt arm. The teddy was sad, but teddy got ready, went to the doctor, was checked, needed a bandage, and then went home feeling much better. The children were provided with materials, so that they could play their own script or copy the idea shown to them by Amity. Children chose a partner to play with. Many children did not separate into groups easily. Amity observed the children play.

At the end of the session, the children came together in a group, but only two groups were able to play and/or describe a story with logical sequences. These two groups worked well together, used object substitution, and demonstrated creativity. Some individuals in other groups were able to describe their own play script but were unable to play with their partner. Some children were focussed on sensory play, feeling the sticky side of plastic strip plasters or wandering the room exploring materials. The "bossy" children were unable to create a logical play script. The child described as "sad" was able to use a laptop prop as an x-ray machine and told a story of the group's visit to hospital in detail. He was told by another child that his x-ray machine was a laptop, not an x-ray machine.

After conducting five play sessions, each with a different emphasis on a play skill, a sixth play session was held, where Amity revisited the first skill of play scripts. Amity presented the teddy, who got ready in the morning, went for a walk, decided to go camping, had lunch, had fun cooking marshmallows as the sun set, looked up at the stars and liked what he saw, got into a spaceship, blasted off into space and landed on the moon, met a kind alien who didn't speak the same language, went home, a little sad, not knowing if he'd see his friend again, brushed his teeth and went to bed thinking about his unusual day. This was a much longer script that included an imagined fictional story with complex object substitutions and all the play skills that the children had learned.

Amity then allowed the class to separate as they wished, and the children were free to create any story they wished. To Amity's surprise, the class separated easily and was immediately on task. One group of three children (including the child described as "bossy") negotiated a script where two princesses were trying to rescue their pet from an evil princess, who had it trapped in a tall tower (a pile of books). They couldn't get across the "moat" (an agreed section of carpet, invisible to everyone but the players). They asked for assistance from a sister and a brother who were sailing on a yacht (a different group of children, two boys with an upturned stool as a yacht). The siblings escorted the princesses across the moat, bid them farewell, and continued on their way.

The siblings then met with a cruise ship (another group of children with a chair) and decided to visit other countries on a cruise, before a number of cruise ship passengers were invited to a sleepover in a teepee by yet another group of children. Players moved from one group, and one story, to the next, seamlessly. Although there was still variation in play abilities, children had the flexibility to adapt to the play level of other players and wanted to include them in their play. The children found great joy in the collaboration and negotiation of new ideas and play possibilities.

Conclusion

Throughout this chapter, we have presented how personal social capabilities reflect a child's ability to create meaning from social interactions, understand verbal and nonverbal communication, and self-regulate. Evidence has been presented to illustrate how personal social capabilities improve the cognitive performance of students, reduce reliance on behaviour management practices, enhance collaborative group work and critical thinking skills of students, and most importantly, improve the quality of friendships and social relationships at school. To nurture these skills and abilities in our classrooms, we can assist children through increasing their pretend play ability. Play is how children communicate, and increased pretend play ability translates into an increased ability to socialise and engage in meaningful interactions with peers and others. Demonstrating metacommunication (by talking about what we and others may be thinking) and introducing objects into the play, assists children to improve their verbal and non-verbal communication skills and understand the intention of others, which supports a child's ability to improve their personal social capabilities.

References

Bruder, M. B., & Chen, L-H. (2007). Measuring social competence in toddlers: Play tools for learning. *Early Childhood Services*, 1(1), 49–70. https://uconnucedd.org/wp-content/uploads/sites/1340/2016/06/MeasSocCompTodd-2007.pdf.

Creaghe, N., Quinn, S., & Kidd, E. (2021). Symbolic play provides a fertile context for language development. *Infancy*. doi:10.1111/infa.12422.

De Haan, D., Vriens-van Hoogdalem, A-G., Zeijlmans, K., & Boom, J. (2021). Meta-communication is social pretend play: Two dimensions. *International Journal of Early Years Education*, 29(4), 405–419. doi:10.1080/09669760.2020.1778451.

Farmer-Dougan, V., & Kaszuba, T. (1999). Reliability and validity of play-based observations: Relationship between the PLAY behaviour observation system and standardised measures of cognitive and social skills. *Educational Psychology*, 16, 429–440. doi:10.1080/0144341990190404.

Gokhale, A. A. (1995). Collaborative learning enhances critical thinking. *Journal of Technology Education*, 7(1), 22–30.

Hughes, C., & Leekam, S. (2004). What are the links between theory of mind and social relations? Review, reflections and new directions for studies of typical and atypical development. *Social Development*, 13(4), 590–619. doi:10.1111/j.1467-9507.2004.00285.x.

Lindsay, E. W., & Colwell, M. J. (2003). Preschoolers' emotional competence: Links to pretend and physical play. *Child Study Journal*, 33, 39–52.

McAloney, K., & Stagnitti, K. (2009). Pretend play and social play: The concurrent validity of the Child-Initiated Pretend Play Assessment. *International Journal of Play Therapy*, 18 (2), 99–113. doi:10.1037/a0014559.

Nicolopoulou, A., Barbosa de Sa, A., Ilgaz, H., & Brockmeyer, C. (2010). Using the transformative power of play to educate hearts and minds: From Vygotsky to Vivian Paley and beyond. *Mind, Culture, and Activity*, 17(1), 42–58. doi:10.1080/10749030903312512.

Rakoczy, H. (2008). Pretence as individual and collective intentionality. *Mind & Language*, 23(5), 499–517. doi:10.1111/j.1468–0017.2008.00357.x.

Stagnitti, K. (2021). Learn to Play Therapy: Principles, process and practical activities. Learn to Play. www.learntoplayevents.com.

Stagnitti, K., Frawley, M., Lynch, B., & Fahey, P. (2013). Increasing social cohesiveness in a school environment. In A. Taket, B. Crisp, M. Graham, L. Hanna, S. Goldinay, & L. Wilson (Eds.), *Practising social inclusion* (pp. 91–105). Routledge.

Stagnitti, K., & Jellie, L. (2023). Play and storytelling. Building literacy skills in the early years. Learn to Play. www.learntoplayevents.com.

Stagnitti, K., & Lewis, F. (2015). The importance of quality of preschool children's pre-tend play ability to the subsequent development of semantic organisation and narrative re-telling skills in early primary school. *International Journal of Speech-Language Pathology*, 17(2), 148–158. doi:10.3109/17549507.2014.941934.

Stagnitti, K., Paatsch, L., Nolan, A., & Campbell, K. (2020). Identifying play skills that predict children's language in the beginning of the first year of school. *Early Years.* doi:10.1080/09575146.2020.1865280.

Uren, N., & Stagnitti, K. (2009). Pretend play, social competence and involvement in children aged 5–7 years: The concurrent validity of the Child-Initiated Pretend Play Assessment. *Australian Occupational Therapy Journal*, 56, 33–40. doi:10.1111/j.1440-1630.2008.00761.x.

Vygotsky, L. S. (2016). Play and its role in the mental development of the child. *International Research in Early Childhood Education*, 7 (2), 3–25. https://files.eric.ed.gov/fulltext/EJ1138861.pdf.

Wallerstedt, C., Pramling, N., & Lagerlöf, P. (2021). Triggering in play: Opening up dimensions of imagination in adult–child play. *Learning, Culture and Social Interaction*, 29, 100497. doi:10.1016/j.Icsi.2021.100497.

Wang, A. T., Lee, S. S., Sigman, M., & Dapretto, M. (2006). Developmental changes in the neural basis of interpreting communicative intent. *SCAN*, 1, 107–121. doi:10.1093/scan/nsl018.

Whitebread, D., & O'Sullivan, L. (2012). Preschool children's social pretend play: Supporting the development of metacommunication, metacognition and self-regulation. *International Journal of Play*, 1, 197–213. doi:10.1080/21594937.2012.693384.

Whittington, V., & Floyd, I. (2009). Creating intersubjectivity during socio-dramatic play at an Australian kindergarten. *Early Child Development and Care*, 179, 143–156.

Ybarra, O., Burnstein, E., Winkielman, P., Keller, M. C., Manis, M., Chan, E., & Rodriguez, J. (2008). Mental exercising through simple socializing: Social interaction promotes general cognitive functioning. *Personality and Social Psychology Bulletin*, 34, 248–259. doi:10.1177/0146167207310454.

Zosh, J. M., Hopkins, E. J., Jensen, H., Liu, C., Neale, D., Hirsh-Pasek, K, Solis, S. L., & Whitebread, D. (2017). *Learning through play: A review of the evidence*. White paper prepared for the LEGO foundation. https://www.legofoundation.com/media/1063/learning-through-play_web.pdf.

Zosh, J. M., Kirsh-Pasek, K., Hopkins, E. J., Jensen, H., Lui, C., Neale, D., Solis, S. L., & Whitebread, D. (2018). Accessing the inaccessible: Redefining play as a spectrum. *Frontiers in Psychology.* https://www.frontiersin.org/articles/10.3389/fpsyg.2018.01124/full.

6 Creative Thinking, Storytelling, and Play

Creative thinking is one of the higher order thinking (HOT) skills needed for 21st century success (Chiruguru, 2020; NebraskaMATH, 2016; Zosh et al., 2018). The other skills are collaboration (see Chapter 5) and communication (see Chapter 3). Creative thinking is expansive, open-ended, trying new approaches, and discovering new possibilities (Chiruguru, 2020; NebraskaMATH, 2016). It has been associated with problem solving, divergent thinking, well-being, and employability (Kirkham & Kidd, 2015). Critical thinking (a fourth skill) is intertwined with creative thinking through divergent thinking, with divergent thinking being the ability to extend beyond one possibility and instead include many (Russ & Wallace, 2013). Storytelling is a form of creativity, as is play, which involves possibilities, creating stories, and being ready for the unexpected (Brown & Vaughan, 2009; Hoffman & Russ, 2012; Stagnitti & Jellie, 2023). In this chapter, we examine the literature on the links between creative thinking, storytelling, and play. The pretend play skills of organisation of play and object substitution will be considered as key components in the development of narrative and creativity, enhancing one's storytelling ability. The chapter concludes with a practical example of a classroom play and storytelling approach in rural Victoria, Australia.

The teacher-centred view in education is that children learn through didactic approaches, allowing for the acquisition of skills and knowledge. This is often pitted against the realms of developmental psychology and Vygotskian perspective, where learning is recognised as more powerful when coming from within the child, developing their cognitive and self-regulation abilities, by improving the quality of their thinking, problem solving skills, and creativity (Nicolopoulou et al., 2006; Whitebread et al., 2009). Teachers who embed pedagogical methods that are conducive to creative thinking create environments that allow opportunities for self-initiated learning and student participation (Hoff & Lemark, 2012). Creating such environments is consistent with the concept of guided play, shown to be more effective for student learning than didactic teaching (Zosh et al., 2018). One reason for its effectiveness is that intentional learning occurs. Intentional learning requires the use of planning, monitoring, and evaluating task performance, which encourages problem solving and creativity. Through intentional learning, metacognitive (thinking about thinking) processes are developed, impacting on learning styles and attitude to learning over the long term (Whitebread et al, 2009).

DOI: 10.4324/9781003296782-7

"Pretend play is a creative act" (Russ & Wallace, 2013, p. 136). Both pretend play and creative thinking share many similar processes, such as divergent thinking, cognitive flexibility, insight, and perspective taking (Russ & Wallace, 2013). In self-initiated pretend play children generate ideas. They create stories that reflect their own lives or ideas of pure fantasy. They use objects as props in the play, understand positive and negative emotions of characters (whether the characters are themselves or a figurine) and imagine the setting of the play (In a boat? On a planet? In a home?). Whilst creating play scenarios, children are negotiating with others to create a shared meaning so the play can be sustained. The children work together to create a narrative, which consists of ordered events and an understanding of how those events might influence the next. The link between creative thinking and pretend play is sustainable over time (Russ & Wallace, 2013), suggesting a sustained play-based approach to support the development of higher order thinking skills, in this case, creativity. A significant component of literacy outcomes within the curriculum is measured around children's ability to create story, both written and oral narratives, alongside their ability to comprehend key components of a narrative. We will now explore the links between creative thinking, storytelling, and play.

Creative thinking, storytelling, and play

Children who engage in pretend play experience joy, pleasure, and emotional intensity when they are truly playing (for example, the excitement of pretend holidays, the stress of fighting a dragon, the contentment of including a toy puppy in the play). Children's involvement in pretend play also provides opportunities to observe how children organise stories or narratives, and how they integrate their emotions with thinking about the story in their play (Russ & Wallace, 2013).

Positive and negative emotions increase creativity because emotions open the mind to search for alternatives and associations (Hoffman & Russ, 2012; Holmes et al., 2019; Russ & Wallace, 2013). During storytelling, the right side of the brain, which is grounded in non-verbal storytelling, makes sense of the whole story experience, processing gestures, sounds, and feelings (Kestly, 2014). This information is sent to the left side of the brain, which expresses the felt experiences through language and re-presents the information in language back to the right side of the brain, where it is processed again to higher levels of metaphor (Kestly, 2014). Metaphor is the symbolic component of play, where meaning is attached to objects, actions, and words to create a true and deeper understanding of the story. This constant back and forth integration between the right and left sides of the brain gives us "a sense of the meaning of the story in our bodies while hearing the story told in words" (Kestly, 2014, p. 121). Children experience this integration when engaging in storytelling through narrative in pretend play (see Chapter 2 for more information on brain function and learning).

Relationships between pretend play, creativity, language, and storytelling have been found in several studies (Holmes et al., 2019). Holmes et al. (2019) explored these relationships with 56 English speaking American children in preschool. They assessed the children with a standardised draw-a-person test, an invitation to children to draw three pictures while telling a story about them (children were instructed to draw a male, a female, and their favourite thing to do) (Holmes et al., 2019). There was also an invitation to children to select a family from five ethnic family doll sets and tell a story (Holmes et al., 2019). These assessments were audio recorded for later analysis. Children were observed for four 10-minute periods during indoor free play with researchers recording the children's play as they played. The play was recorded and analysed by social indicators (onlooker, solitary, dyadic, and group) and type of play (arts and crafts, tabletop play, constructive play, games with rules, pretend play, puzzles) (Holmes et al., 2019). Children were also given a standardised language assessment. The results indicated strong connections between pretend play and verb use in storytelling, with children in the social play group using more adjectives and prepositions. Arts and crafts play was connected to language and the authors argued that arts and crafts and pretend play share some cognitive processes (Holmes et al., 2019). Children who enjoyed drawing were expressive in their storytelling. Onlooker play and tabletop play were related to less language and lower creativity (Holmes et al., 2019). This study found that the type of play in a classroom was important for creativity, with pretend play and arts and crafts being connected to language and creativity in storytelling (Holmes et al., 2019).

Hoffman and Russ (2012) explored connections between creativity, pretend play, emotion regulation, and executive function in a group of 61 girls aged 5–10 years with a mean age of 7.4 years. Forty-nine of the 61 children were in primary school. Children were seen during two lunch breaks to complete the Affect in Play Scale (Russ, 2004), a card-sorting task to test executive function, a storytelling task with a wordless book to test creativity in storytelling, and an alternative uses task, to test divergent thinking (Hoffman & Russ, 2012). A vocabulary test from an IQ assessment was used to measure verbal intelligence and parents were sent a checklist for emotional regulation to complete on their child (Hoffman & Russ, 2012). The results found positive emotional processes in pretend play were significantly related to higher storytelling scores in story likability, creativity, and imagination. Children who were rated as more imaginative in their pretend play told more creative stories (Hoffman & Russ, 2012, p. 180).

Despite children having less time in unstructured play, Russ found that over two decades of research from 1985 to 2008, 894 children aged 6–10 years did not reduce their level of organisation of the play story and the amount and range of emotional expression in their play stories (Russ & Dillon, 2011). Casey (2017) carried out a longitudinal study in Australia from 2009 to 2011 with 26 children who were rated by their preschool teachers to be resilient. The study followed children from preschool to their second year of formal learning (children were aged 5–7 years). One of the measures used was the Child-Initiated Pretend Play Assessment (Stagnitti, 2022), which measures the complexity of children's spontaneous initiation in pretend play through scoring elaborate play action sequences and object substitution. The elaborate scores are indicative of children's ability to create complex logical sequences of play that are reflective of narrative ability.

Casey (2017) found that the most significant change in overall complexity of play ability occurred from the first year of formal schooling to the second year of formal schooling (from ages 6 to 7 years). By the second year of schooling the participants were very capable of actively engaging in their learning at an advanced participation level, rather than returning to managing routines and teacher-led group learning. Casey's findings have implications for how play is embedded in the classroom. For example, excessively scripted classroom play corners created by teachers that have specific themes to teach vocabulary associated with the play activities, have proven in practice to have limited educational benefits because they do not provide enough scope for children's own initiatives and creativity (Nicolopoulou et al., 2010).

An example of embedding play and storytelling in the classroom that motivates children to learn and allows children to extend and initiate their own creative thinking is Vivian Paley's work in storytelling and story-acting practice (Nicolopoulou et al., 2010). Storytelling is narrative. Nicolopoulou et al. (2010) noted that narrative ability is a continuum from discursive exposition (storytelling) to enactment of the story (pretend play). In Nicolopoulou et al.'s (2010) study, it was the *telling and acting* of the story that was critical to this approach being effective. Essentially this approach involves children who wish to dictate a story going to a teacher who writes down the story as the child tells it (the teacher does no editing). Later that day, the story is read aloud to the whole class by the teacher while the child (author of the story) and other children chosen by the child/author, act out the story (Nicolopoulou et al., 2010). The children's storytelling is self-initiated. The teacher's role is facilitative, in that, teachers transcribe and read out the children's story with the aim to establish, maintain, and facilitate child-initiated storytelling. Over a 2-year study in the USA, a group comparison study was undertaken. Eighty-one children were involved in storytelling and story acting in their classrooms and 66 children did not have the program in their school. Those children in the storytelling and story acting schools participated in the program twice a week for 6–7 months and composed and acted out 553 child-initiated stories (Nicolopoulou et al., 2010). In contrast to the children who did not have the program, all children in the storytelling and story acting group significantly improved in overall story comprehension skills, with improved print and word awareness, increased social competence, self-regulation, and reduced social disruption (Nicolopoulou et al., 2010).

Object substitution, creative or divergent thinking

In 1973 and 1975, Dansky and Silverman carried out research studies on object use and creative thinking (also called associative fluency or divergent thinking). In their 1973 study 90 children were placed in one of four groups. Group 1 played with four objects; group 2 imitated four behaviours of an adult using the objects; and group 3 coloured some pictures. They found that group 1 children were better at associative fluency tests, which indicated creative thinking. In 1975, they found that if children played with unstructured materials, children's subsequence divergent problem solving improved. In 1999, Russ et al. carried out a 4-year follow up study of 31 children from an original sample of 121 children. They found that the quality of children's pretend play from four years previously predicted the children's divergent thinking, independent of the child's IQ (Russ et al., 1999).

"Divergent thinking is especially important in creative production" (Hoffman & Russ, 2012, p. 175). Divergent thinking is fluidity of thinking that can go in different directions (Holmes et al., 2019, p. 244). The development of divergent thinking is supported through object substitution in pretend play, with object substitution being the ability to use an object as if it were something else (Stagnitti, 2002). An example of object substitution would be using a box for a car or a shoe as a phone. Object substitution requires the suspension of reality, counterfactual reasoning, and is evidence of representational thought, allowing for the development of divergent and abstract thinking (Francis and Gibson, 2023; Russ, 2004; Stagnitti, 2002; Zosh et al., 2018).

Stagnitti (2002) carried out a study to test the theoretical link between creative thinking, playfulness, and object substitution. There were 80 5-year-old children in the study, which included 40 children whose teachers were concerned about their pre-academic ability. The children's object substitution ability was measured with the Child-Initiated Pretend Play Assessment (ChIPPA) (Stagnitti, 2022), playfulness was measured using Lieberman's Playfulness Scale (Lieberman, 1977) and divergent thinking was measured using the Associative Fluency Test (Ward, 1968). Object substitution was significantly related to divergent thinking (r = .33, $p < .01$) and playfulness (r = .4, $p < .001$) (Stagnitti, 2002). This study provided empirical evidence for a relationship between using objects as something else in pretend play, enjoyment of play (playfulness), and creative thinking (divergent problem solving). This study supports Russ's research where enjoyment in pretend play, which includes the skill of object substitution, is related to creative thinking.

Casey's (2017) longitudinal study found that children's increasing ability to use divergent thinking was closely linked to the increasing complexity of their elaborate play using unstructured objects. The ability to use unstructured materials (such as boxes, cloth, dowel, and tin) within a play story is evidence of divergent thinking, the ability to be free and fluid with thinking and to generate a variety of ideas. By 7 years of age, children had increased in their ability to create stories with the unstructured objects in the ChIPPA by using abstract thought and divergent thinking.

Children who were creative and novel story tellers in Hoffman and Russ's (2012) study were the children who could think of alternative uses of objects that were unique compared to other children (that is, divergent thinking). Hoffman and Russ (2012) also found that children who showed higher levels of organisation and imagination in their pretend play could generate more alternative responses on a divergent thinking task, which was independent of verbal ability. They also found that children who showed a variety of emotions in their puppet play were also better at divergent thinking.

Apart from divergent thinking ability, children's object substitution ability in pretend play has been significantly related to a child's social competence (Uren &

Stagnitti, 2009), with children who lack this play ability being socially disruptive with peers. In a study by Casey et al. (2012) on the early peer play relationships of children identified as resilient, significant positive correlations were found between the children's ability to produce object substitutions in play and their level of play interaction as assessed by preschool teacher reports. In a group of children in their first year of formal learning, children's ability to substitute objects in pretend play predicted their language ability (Stagnitti et al., 2020) and a 4-year follow up study found that children's object substitution ability at 4 and 5 years of age was influential in their narrative re-tell ability four years later (Stagnitti & Lewis, 2015). Positive play interactions involve the ability to use both receptive and expressive language skills in play, to extend the play through forward and logical thinking, to be creative in play, and display positive emotion, encouraging others to join in play by negotiation (Casey et al., 2012).

Divergent thinking suggests children are able to understand the play ideas of their peers and how play objects can be represented by someone else as different to their own perceptions (Russ, 2004). The ability to generate a variety of ideas in response to a problem also suggests an ability to cope with stressful events or circumstances through the capacity for flexible thinking (Russ, 2004). As children develop skills for creativity and problem solving, they are better able to draw on coping skills to manage daily situations (Christiano & Russ, 1996).

Practical resources and a classroom example of creative thinking, storytelling, and play

A practical resource for play and storytelling for teachers is *Play and Storytelling: Building Literacy Skills in the Early Years* by Stagnitti and Jellie (2023). This book has 45 play activities linked to storytelling. These activities can be used in the classroom, and there are printable proformas to support some activities. For children who have challenging social issues, Sherratt and Donald (2004) and Goldingay et al. (2020) provide detailed information on programs that have been found to develop storytelling and social connection for children up to 15 years who have challenging behaviours.

To conclude this chapter, we present an example of a play and storytelling approach that was carried out in a rural primary school in Australia. The approach was led by Siobhan Casey, initially with teacher involvement in each of the sessions. The storytelling and play approach consisted of the following. The school had adopted an approach in which the children from foundation level through to Year 2 were participating in group-based storytelling and play sessions, using unstructured (box, cloth, tin, sticks, cloth doll, pebbles) objects only. Siobhan would model the potential narrative to the class for that session, and the children were encouraged to consider a similar beginning and ending; however, children were encouraged to draw on their collective creativity to change and shape the middle of their narrative. The children did so in groups, where a scaffolding or guided play approach was used to support their storytelling. This approach was used weekly over the course of the year. Throughout the year different story books supported the skeleton of the play scenario, which then went on to support the exploration of language and literacy skills in the classroom.

Here is an example of one of the many positive student outcomes related to the storytelling and play approach. After the play and storytelling sessions, at the end of the term, parents of a child in Year 2 (8 years old) approached Siobhan, praising the play and storytelling work that had been carried out within the classroom. Her daughter had written a narrative based around the indigenous story *Big Rain Coming* by Katrina Germein and illustrated by Bronwyn Bancroft. This book provided the skeleton of the narrative Siobhan had modelled to this class in one of the sessions with the unstructured objects. Within the storytelling and play approach, this child had experienced connecting emotion in play with others, exploring the language use around the story in a play space with peers, and drawing on a collective creative approach to developing their story. She had written a piece that had far exceeded her previous ability and left both parents and educators in awe of the work she had produced. Her piece included detail around the beginning, middle, and end of the story. She had used verbs and adjectives in describing the characters' motivations and actions, giving rise to the opportunity for her to explore punctuation use. There was a sense of understanding around the emotion of finally experiencing some rain in the story. Through her writing, a true understanding of the use of language was evident.

By physically manipulating the objects in negotiation with her peers to create and organise a story, this child had explored sound, gesture, feelings, and processed non-verbal communication around the story. The skeleton of the narrative had been previously modelled by Siobhan and this provided a necessary support to those children who found organising a story in play difficult. Within this child's group, all children had experienced the anticipation around what their story might look like. They came together, discussed, and negotiated what each of the unstructured objects would represent in their story and began using their skills of creativity, divergent thinking, and representation, working together to organise their story.

The positive emotion and anticipation around the story provided the opportunity for right-brain connection and exploration within the group, that being processing of non-verbal, sound, gestural, and body language, to create a shared experience. Siobhan joined the group and passively observed their organisation. With the skills of encouraging child-initiated exploration and thinking, Siobhan was able to use descriptive language and questioning to guide their thinking. This shifted the storytelling and narrative development process to the left brain, supporting the connection of language around the felt experience of creating a collective story. Following this level of scaffolding Siobhan then tracked the group's story, encouraging the children to shift back into the metaphor and enjoy the process of playing out and developing their story with a collective creative approach. Pretend play offered an opportunity for each of the children to explore their individual skills for creativity, divergent thinking, and organisation of play. Doing this in a collective provided further opportunity for self-regulation, social competence, and deeper emotional understanding of the story experience.

Conclusion

Siegel (2012), states that integration between emotions and cognition in the brain not only supports higher intelligence, but also supports greater connection, flexibility, creativity, and adaptability through increased positive emotion. Storytelling integrates the right and left sides of the brain and is connected to creativity. Telling and acting out a story in play has been shown to increase children's story comprehension, and using unstructured objects within a play scenario is related to divergent thinking and later narrative re-tell ability.

When using symbols in play, attributing properties, making reference to absent objects or logically and sequentially organising a play scenario, children are being creative and solving problems, developing metacognitive processes (Whitebread et al. 2009; Russ, 2004). Through problem solving and creativity in learning, children are developing the skill of divergent thinking.

Children experience a feeling of joy and pleasure through the autonomy of creating beyond limitations. The "what if" in play provides an opportunity for the development of curiosity, further sparking greater motivation to engage in learning, and this process is even more powerful when creating within a collective. The lifelong benefits of establishing self-regulatory skills when negotiating and cooperating within a group are significant parameters of health and wellbeing for children.

References

Brown, S., & Vaughan, C. (2009). *Play. How it shapes the brain, opens the imagination, and invigorates the soul.* Penguin.

Casey, S. (2017). Resilience in early years: Understanding pretend play and self-regulation development. Unpublished doctoral thesis. Deakin University, Geelong, Australia.

Casey, S., Stagnitti, K., Taket, A., & Nolan, A. (2012). Early peer play interactions of resilient children living in disadvantaged communities. *International Journal of Play*, 3, 311–323. doi:10.1080/21594937.2012.741432.

Chiruguru, S. B. (2020). The essential skills of the 21st Century Classroom (4Cs). Research paper. https://www.researchgate.net/profile/Suresh-Chiruguru/publication/340066140_The_Essential_Skills_of_21st_Century_Classroom_4Cs/links/5e75277d4585157b9a4d9964/The-Essential-Skills-of-21st-Century-Classroom-4Cs.pdf.

Christiano, B., & Russ, S. (1996). Play as a predictor of coping and distress in children during an invasive dental procedure. *Journal of Clinical Child Psychology*, 25, 130–138. doi:10.1207/s15374424jccp2502_1.

Dansky, J. L., & Silverman, I. W. (1973). Effects of play on associative fluency in preschool aged children. *Developmental Psychology*, 9, 38–43.

Dansky, J. L., & Silverman, I. W. (1975). Play: A general facilitator of associative fluency. *Developmental Psychology*, 11, 104.

Francis, G. A., & Gibson, J. L. (2023). A plausible role of imagination in pretend play, counterfactual reasoning, and executive functions. *British Journal of Psychology*, 3 March, 1–22. doi:10.1111/bjop.12650.

Goldingay, S., Stagnitti, K., Dean, B., Robertson, N., Davidson, D., & Francis, E. (2020). *Storying beyond social difficulties for neuro-diverse adolescents: The Imagine Create Belong social development program.* Routledge.

Hoff, E., & Lemark, E. (2012). Critical creative moments in Swedish classrooms. In R. Jacobs (Ed.), *Creative engagements with children: International perspectives and contexts* (pp. 33–41). Brill.

Hoffman, J., & Russ, S. (2012). Pretend play, creativity, and emotion regulation in children. *Psychology of Aesthetics, Creativity and the Arts*, 6, 175–184. doi:10.1037/a0026299.

Holmes, R.M., Gardner, B., Kohm, K., Bant, C., Ciminello, A., Moedt, K., & Romeo, L. (2019). The relationship between young children's language abilities, creativity, play and storytelling. *Early Child Development and Care*, 189, 244–254. doi:10.1080/03004430.2017.1314274.

Kestly, T. (2014). *The interpersonal neurobiology of play*. W. W. Norton.

Kirkham, J., & Kidd, E. (2015). The effect of Steiner, Montessori, and National Curriculum education upon children's pretence and creativity. *Journal of Creative Behavior*, 51, 20–34. doi:10.1002/jocb.83.

Lieberman, J. N. (1977). *Playfulness*. Academic Press.

NebraskaMATH (2016). Thoughtful learning: What are the 4 C's of learning skills? https://newsroom.unl.edu/announce/csmce/5344/29195.

Nicolopoulou, A., Barbosa de Sá, A., Ilgaz, H., & Brockmeyer, C. (2010). Using the transformative power of play to educate hearts and minds: From Vygotsky to Vivian Paley and beyond. *Mind, Culture, and Activity*, 17, 42–58. doi:10.1080/10749030903312512.

Nicolopoulou, A., McDowell, J., & Brockmeyer, C. (2006). Narrative play and emergent literacy: Storytelling and story-acting meet journal writing. In D. Singer., R. Golinkoff & K. Hirsh-Pasek (Eds.), *Play = learning: How play motivates and enhances children's cognitive and social-emotional growth* (pp. 124–144). Oxford University Press.

Russ, S. (2004). *Play in child development and psychotherapy: Toward empirically supported practice*. Lawrence Erlbaum.

Russ, S., & Dillon, J. (2011). Changes in children's pretend play over two decades. *Creativity Research Journal*, 23, 330–338. doi:10.1080/10400419.2011.621824.

Russ, S., Robins, A., & Christiano, B. (1999). Pretend play: Longitudinal prediction of creativity and affect in fantasy in children. *Creativity Research Journal*, 12, 129–139.

Russ, S., & Wallace, C. (2013). Pretend play and creative process. *American Journal of Play*, 6, 136–148.

Sherratt, D., & Donald, G. (2004). Connectedness: Developing a shared construction of affect and cognition in children with autism. *British Journal of Special Education*, 31, 10–15.

Siegel, D. (2012). *The developing mind* (2nd edn). Guilford Press.

Stagnitti, K. (2022). *The Child-Initiated Pretend Play Assessment 2* (2nd edn). Learn to Play. www.learntoplaytherapy.com.

Stagnitti, K. (2002). The development of a child-initiated pretend play assessment. Unpublished doctoral thesis. LaTrobe University, Melbourne, Australia.

Stagnitti, K., & Jellie, L. (2023). Play and storytelling: Building literacy skills in the early years. Learn to Play. www.learntoplaytherapy.com.

Stagnitti, K., & Lewis, F. (2015). The importance of the quality of preschool children's pretend play ability to the subsequent development of semantic organisation and narrative re-telling skills in early primary school. *International Journal of Speech-Language Pathology*, 17, 148–158. doi:10.3109/17549507.2014.941934.

Stagnitti, K., Paatsch, L., Nolan, A., & Campbell, K. (2020). Identifying play skills that predict children's language in the beginning of the first year of school. Early Years. doi:10.1080/09575146.2020.1865280.

Uren, N., & Stagnitti, K. (2009). Pretend play, social competence and involvement in children aged 5–7 years: The concurrent validity of the Child-Initiated Pretend Play Assessment. *Australian Occupational Therapy Journal*, 56(1), 33–40. doi:10.1111/j.1440-1630.2008.00761.x.

Ward, W. (1968). Creativity in young children. *Child Development*, 39, 737–754.

Whitebread, D., Coltman, P., Jameson, H., & Lander, R. (2009). Play, cognition and self-regulation: What exactly are children learning when they learn through play? *Educational and Child Psychology*, 26, 40–52.

Zosh, J., Hirsh-Pasek, K., Hopkins, E., Jensen, H., Liu, C., Neale, D., Solis, L., & Whitebread, D. (2018). Assessing the inaccessible: Redefining play as a spectrum. *Frontiers in Psychology*, 9, 1–12. doi:10.3389/fpsyg.2018.01124.

Section 2

The How

7 Play Is Not an Add On

Rather a Way of Doing

In the early 1700s, Jean Jacques Rousseau, a philosopher and composer of music, so aptly stated "Don't force the child to learn, create a desire in [them] to want to learn" (Wilkinson, 2004, p. 263). We argue that play provides a rich and authentic environment for children to be motivated to learn.

Play is a central tenet of early childhood education and is strongly embedded in teacher practices to support children's cognitive, academic, social, and emotional learning (Jay & Knaus, 2018; Nolan & Paatsch, 2018; Parker et al., 2022). In Australia, play-based learning in preschools is entrenched in mandated national and state government early learning frameworks, such as the *Belonging, Being & Becoming: Early Years Learning Framework for Australia* (EYLF, Australian Government Department of Education, Employment and Workplace Relations, 2009) and the *Victorian Early Years Learning Framework* (VEYLDF, Department of Education and Training, 2016). In the contexts of formal schooling, policy makers, educators, and researchers are beginning to understand the importance of including play-based learning approaches within the school curriculum. However, introducing a play-based approach, while also meeting the demands of the crowded curriculum, can often be challenging for some teachers (Nolan & Paatsch, 2018; Parker et al., 2022). Over the years we have worked with many teachers in primary schools as they begin their journey to embed a play-based learning approach in their classrooms. Initially, some teachers report tensions such as:

> Is this another add-on in an already crowded curriculum?
>
> How will I fit my literacy block into the day if I have to add in play? How will they learn writing in play?
>
> How do we see the learning, and how do children meet the outcomes in the Australian Curriculum?

However, within a short period of time, teachers begin to see the value of play and the ways that learning through play occurs, alongside meeting curriculum outcomes within these play experiences.

This chapter sets out to demystify some of these tensions in the pursuit of innovative pedagogical methods by illustrating ways in which play provides a rich and authentic environment to support these learning outcomes. Play is framed

DOI: 10.4324/9781003296782-9

here as *not* an add on, but rather a way of doing. We also present some practical examples of innovative ways that schools have incorporated play into classrooms to support children's learning outcomes in all learning areas of the curriculum, as well as across the general capabilities and cross curriculum priorities.

Situating play across the Australian Curriculum

One of the main aims for the design of the Australian Curriculum was to support all "young Australians to become successful learners, confident and creative individuals, and active and informed citizens" (Australian Curriculum, Assessment and Reporting Authority [ACARA], 2020). Given the extensive research evidence, in the areas of psychology, anthropology, education, health, and neuroscience, which has shown that learning through play has a significant influence on children's overall learning and development, we argue that guided play informs pedagogical practice and should be taken seriously as an effective medium to support long term learning outcomes for children alongside greater child–teacher connection.

Figure 7.1 presents a representation of one way to conceptualise the interconnectedness between play and the curriculum. Specifically, play is situated as a context for achieving curriculum learning outcomes, general capabilities, and cross-curriculum priorities as well as the children's play abilities. Together, this representation supports the notion of play as a way of doing, not an add on.

Link between play and the Australian Curriculum Learning Areas and General Capabilities

As outlined in the Australian Curriculum, disciplinary knowledge skills and understandings are described in the eight Learning Areas, while the General Capabilities are addressed through the content of the Learning Areas (ACARA, 2020).

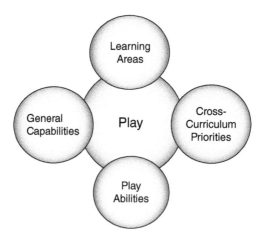

Figure 7.1 Interconnectedness between play and the Australian Curriculum

There is a large body of research that has explored the relationship between children's play and academic skills that align to the Australian Curriculum Learning Areas, including English, mathematics, science, the arts, and technologies (Creaghe et al., 2021; Hirsh-Pasek et al., 2009; Hollenstein et al., 2022; Quinn et al., 2018). In addition, research has also shown that play fosters children's critical thinking, creativity, social and emotional development, problem-solving, ethical understandings (see Chapters 4–6), and digital processing knowledge (Hollenstein et al., 2022). These skills align closely to the General Capabilities outlined in the Australian Curriculum. The following sections will present some examples of research that demonstrate the links between play and these skills in young children.

The English learning area in the Australian Curriculum is organised into three interrelated strands: Language, Literature, and Literacy, to support students to analyse, communicate effectively, build relationships with others, and to "listen to, view, speak, write, create, and reflect on increasingly complex and sophisticated spoken, written, and multimodal texts" (ACARA, 2020). As outlined in Chapter 3, it is well established that there is a strong link between play and language. For example, in a recent Australian study by Stagnitti et al. (2020) exploring a group of 5- to 6-year-old children in their first year of schooling, results showed that the play skill of object substitution predicted a child's receptive and expressive language. Furthermore, research has shown that there is a strong link between children's play and social and emotional development – abilities related to pragmatic language skills (i.e., the social use of language). These pragmatic skills involve taking turn, asking questions, maintaining a topic, and creating narrative (see Chapter 3). Such abilities are also strongly aligned to many of the General Capabilities such as personal and social capabilities (see Chapters 4 and 5), as well as ethical understanding, and literacy.

The link between play and literacy skills is also evident in the research. For example, Wilkinson and Rike (1993) described guided symbolic dramatic play as the missing link to literacy. Holmes et al. (2022) found positive interactions between play and drawing creativity and play and story creativity in 151 children aged 4–6 years. Similarly, Yoon (2014) found that play provided a rich environment for purposeful writing. In a more recent study by Moedt and Holmes (2020) that explored the reading comprehension skills of 42 children aged 5–6 years, results showed that the children who engaged in purposeful guided play scored significantly higher in story sequencing and understanding characters and plots, compared with children who were not in play. Similar links between play and early literacy skills were also reported in a study by Cavanaugh et al. (2017) where children's engagement in guided play supported their development of phonics and phonological awareness, new vocabulary, story composition, and sequences of ideas that demonstrated understanding of complex cause and effect. Other studies have also shown that children's sequences of temporal-causal events and narrative abilities were also enhanced in play compared to non-play contexts (see Chapter 3 for a more detailed discussion).

Rich and authentic guided play environments also provide opportunities for children to learn mathematical concepts. Dockett and Perry (2010) suggest that many children demonstrate mathematical ideas and explorations during play but highlight the need for teachers to have strong mathematical knowledge, and an understanding of the ways that children's mathematical thinking and learning can be supported, including an understanding of their own role in the play. Worthington and van Oers (2016) explored children's mathematical concepts and graphics (representations, personal marks, and mathematical symbols) during pretend play episodes. Teachers were invited to write ongoing observations of the children's mathematical concepts and graphics during play. Findings showed that over 44% of the play episodes included children's use of some mathematics within their play, including money, time, weight, temperature, length, and distance; and over 46% where children spontaneously used their mathematical graphics to communicate (e.g., symbols to represent quantities) (p. 62).

The Science learning area in the Australian Curriculum aims to develop students' understandings of the nature of scientific enquiry, and the ability to solve problems, to communicate scientific understandings, to expand their curiosity, to speculate and ask questions. Again, we argue that play is a rich context for such skills and abilities to be fostered. As discussed in previous sections of this book, there is a strong link between children's play abilities and their problem-solving skills. For example, in a recent study by Hollenstein and colleagues (2022) children's problem-solving skills in a pretend play scenario of an IT centre were explored. The children were able to identify problems (e.g., "my cellphone is broken"), analyse the problem, create a plan to solve the problem, carry out the plan, then evaluate the outcome. In addition, this group of children often initiated the problem and the reason for the problem (e.g., "the phone is not working because it's broken"), while teachers expanded on the child's initiation to support the children's understanding of digital processing (e.g., "is that because there is no wi-fi connection?"). These findings also demonstrate the importance of guided pretend play in supporting children's digital processes and digital play, and how such opportunities can foster children's abilities to communicate, investigate, and create with information and communication technology – another area of the General Capabilities outlined in the Australian Curriculum.

Let's now have a look at an example from the context of the classroom and explore the ways in which play provides opportunities for teachers to observe children's learning across the Curriculum Learning Areas and the General Capabilities in the Australian Curriculum.

Two teachers, Matt and Jonathon, were investigating the types of digital use in children's homes. They invited the Year 1 children to make items that represented any forms of the digital from their homes using a variety of materials including boxes, coloured paper, string, textas, stickers, and paint. Some children had made phones, decorating them with stickers and drawings to represent the apps on the phone. Other children decorated their phones using pebbles and glitter to represent their colourful phone cases. Children also made iPads, computers, remote controls, fridges with touch screens, and voice activated devices used in the home to assist with household tasks such as turning on lights, operating coffee machines etc. These items were then used in the children's play in the classroom.

Table 7.1 presents an excerpt from the first 10–15 minutes of a play scene that the children developed collaboratively. During this part of the play, Matt observed

Table 7.1 The links between children's play and aspects of the Australian Curriculum

Observed child interactions	Examples of links to the Learning Areas (LA) & General Capabilities (GC)	Play skills (PPCT; Stagnitti & Paatsch, 2018)
One group of five children gathered a small table, chairs, and a box of concrete and abstract objects, including cups, plates, sticks, fabric, boxes, papers, and pens and began to set up the scene as an Indian restaurant.	LA English: Creating literature – setting up the scene for a narrative GC Social Management: Working collaboratively	Play Script: Story starting to reflect life in and out of the home
Two children, Elijah and Krishav, folded paper as menus and decided on which items to include on the menu, sharing their experiences of eating Indian food. They decided on butter chicken, rice, lamb korma and naan bread, and described these dishes to the other three children – Bella, Sarah, and Tao.	LA English: Creating literature – negotiated props for the narrative LA English: Language for interaction – expressing and developing ideas GC Social Management: Working collaboratively and share experiences	Play Script: Building on story to include props Sequences of play action starting to appear
Tao and Bella set up some large boxes as the kitchen and counter, while Sarah announced her role as the waitress. This announcement created conflict between her and Tao as they both wanted to play the role. Negotiation, turn-taking, and providing a rationale for why each child wanted the role ensued. Eventually the problem was resolved with some assistance from Bella, who suggested that one could be the chef and the other could be the waitress. Sarah was happy to be the chef.	LA English: Language for interaction, including verbal and non-verbal GC Social Management: Negotiate and resolve conflict, developing leadership skills, communicating effectively GC Social Awareness: Appreciate diverse perspectives and understanding relationships	Role Play: Establishment of roles and role negotiation
Bella decided to join Elijah and Krishav at the table to play the role of the customer. Bella went to find a handbag and proceeded to fill it with her phone and other abstract objects (fabric pieces and a block), narrating what she was doing to the other children, and pretending to put on lipstick with the small block.	LA English: Creating literature, establishing props and characters in the narrative LA English: Literacy – creating text LA Language: Metacommunication	Sequences of Play Action: different actions in a logical sequence Object Substitution: block for lipstick Digital Play: Using a pretend phone

Observed child interactions	Examples of links to the Learning Areas (LA) & General Capabilities (GC)	Play skills (PPCT; Stagnitti & Paatsch, 2018)
Elijah, Krishav, and Bella looked at the menus and started to talk about what they were going to order. Elijah realised there were no drinks on the menu and called for the waiter, saying "what about drinks?" Tao could see the problem and told the customers they could go to the fridge and press the screen to order their drink [he pointed to absent object and pretended to press]. He also said that they had to order their food using the QR code. Krishav realised there were no QR codes on the table so picked up a block and told the others that it was the QR code. Bella took out her phone and waved it over the block. Krishav and Elijah did the same.	LA English: Creating literature. Problems appearing in the play as well as resolutions. There is a set of logical sequences to the story. GC ICT: Understanding ICT systems and digital technologies	Digital Play: tapping screen, use of QR codes Play Script: Story reflecting real life where further problems appear that are resolved Sequences of Play Actions: continued detailed logical sequences of actions Object Substitution: use of block
Tao had not realised that the orders had been made because he was busy setting up the iPad on the counter. He cut a piece of string and stuck one end on the iPad and another to a box. Sarah was busy getting the cooking materials ready. Krishav commented to Bella and Elijah that he was hungry and that the waiter needed to hurry and come to the table. Bella agreed and said that she might have to find another restaurant (both looking sad).	LA English: Creating literature. Adding props and continuing to build the narrative LA Language: Language for interaction. Taking the perspective of another (pragmatics and Theory of Mind). Expressing and developing ideas GC Self-awareness: Recognising and understanding emotions	Digital play Play Script: adding props. Story reflecting real life where further problems appear that are resolved Sequences of Play Actions
Tao heard this then went to the table to talk to his customers. He said, "So sorry, but the iPad is flat. I have just plugged it in to charge. I will have to take your order" and went back to get the paper and pen. Tao then writes the order for "2 nan bred", "2 buta tiken" and "1 lam kormar". Tao looks at his wrist, pretends to tap a watch, then says "it should be working in 5 minutes".	LA English: Phonics and word knowledge LA Language: Cause and effect LA Mathematics: Number, time, and problem-solving, cause and effect LA English: Creating literature – problem and resolution GC Self-awareness: Recognising and understanding emotions GC ICT: Understanding ICT systems and digital technologies	Digital Play Play Script: adding props. Story reflecting real life where further problems appear that are resolved

this group of children without joining in the play. In the first column of this table a description of our observations of the interactions is outlined, including some of the dialogue between the children. In the second column we present examples of the links to some of the Australian Curriculum Learning Areas and General Capabilities to demonstrate the learning through the play. The third column includes a description of the key play skills evident in these interactions, including digital play. The play skills use descriptors from the five play skills outlined in the Pretend Play Checklist for Teachers (PPCT; Stagnitti & Paatsch, 2018) (see Chapter 10 for details of the PPCT assessment tool).

The play scenario continued for another 20 minutes with children working collaboratively to develop their narrative. During this time, Jonathon took photos of the children in their play. Matt took on different roles to guide the play and to support children's learning (see Chapter 9 for further discussion on the role of the teacher). For example, Matt noted that Sarah had not contributed any new ideas to the group narrative in her role as the chef. She stood and moved plates and cups around on top of a box. Matt took on the role as co-player and entered the play scene as another chef. He told Sarah that he was a new chef at the restaurant and wanted to know about the order and what to cook. Together they interacted with the other children and provided further problems and resolutions to the narrative. The following day, the children were shown the photos from the play scene and invited to use them to create a narrative text in digital form.

This excerpt shows an example of how children's language, literacy, mathematics, ICT, and play skills were supported during guided play. The teachers observed, modelled, scaffolded, and co-constructed the narrative with the children throughout the play. They provided a rich and authentic learning environment that supported the achievement of Curriculum Learning Areas and General Capabilities outlined in the Australian Curriculum, during and after the play.

Let's look at another example of how play is embedded in teachers' practices to support older children to achieve learning outcomes outlined in the Australian Curriculum. St James Parish Primary School, Victoria, has implemented play-based learning within a transformative model of learning throughout a process that spans 17 years. Their whole-school approach to curriculum design adopts an "Understanding by Design" (Wiggins et al., 2005) that embeds the underpinning principles of play within this process. The school starts with the curriculum's desired outcomes then asks, "What learning support will students need in order to achieve these outcomes?" and "What are the 'big ideas' for each year level from a subject area?" For example, in the Year 4/5 class the big idea was "to change life, we must first change space". Figure 7.2 presents the big ideas generated by the teachers for the Year 4/5 classes. There are five projects in total, each encouraging students to think from different perspectives. The students build a storyboard to develop a place where all are at peace, considering all perspectives as they engage in the projects.

In this example, there are principles of play evident, demonstrating how a guided play approach merges with the curriculum outcomes. For example, a guided play framework at this level would involve students initiating ideas, developing characters with different perspectives, negotiating roles (e.g., government,

"To change life, we must first change space"
Henri Lefebvre, French writer

Ever since ancient times, civilizations have attempted to plan cities in order to make them work better. Planners seek to organize a city so that it benefits all its inhabitants. They do things such as **build housing, construct infrastructure** like roads and plumbing, provide **public services** like electricity and garbage collection, coordinate commerce, **provide recreational facilities** such as parks, stadiums and museums, and facilitate transport.

These days, planning is not a simple job suited for one department or group. More and more, the cooperation of a number of government departments, local organizations and private citizens is needed to make a city, even a neighbourhood, function healthily. Nevertheless, a coherent vision of what is necessary, what is good and what works is needed if cities are going to survive in the future.

In this Dilemma you have been employed by the United Governments of the World to research, design and build a model city of the future. As you progress through each stage of your city's formation you will also be involved with daily life experiences through 'The Storyboard.' Each of these experiences has enormous privileges attached, however you will only earn these if you can apply what you have learnt in the projects to 'The Game.' **There are five projects in total.** Each project is divided into thinking from a number of different perspectives. You are required to complete **at least one activity from each perspective** however the more understanding you have the more value you will have in the game. Remember at every stage of this Dilemma one rule applies, **live long and be at peace.** Good Luck!

Figure 7.2 The Big Ideas project within a Year 4/5 classroom. Used with permission by Peter Fahey, co-principal, St James Parish School.

local organisations, and private citizens), sequencing actions and events to create a narrative (e.g., merging the building of houses, recreational facilities and public services to create a peaceful coherent place), and being able to generate problems/hypotheses (e.g., as they engage in different projects, each with different perspectives, problems arise). As the students continue to create their storyboard throughout the term they would be engaging in complex interactions in and out of the roles they play – roles can often be conflicted (e.g., verbalising their own perspectives versus reporting from the perspective of their role as a person advocating the building of roads over the building of a park). Consideration is also given to the use of unstructured objects within the play as they build their city that is transformed to represent people, buildings, parks, roads, electricity, and commerce. Together these play principles link to the outcomes in all Learning Areas and the General Capabilities outlined in the Australian Curriculum.

As previously stated, there are several mandated curriculum guidelines and learning frameworks that are implemented across Australia. We have explored the Australian Curriculum to illustrate ways curriculum outcomes can link to play. However, teachers working with children in the early years of schooling are also required to implement the early years framework due to its focus on children from birth to 8 years. In the following section we provide examples of ways in which play can support learning outcomes described in both the Victorian Early Years Learning Development Framework (VEYLDF; Department of Education and Training, Victoria, 2016) and the national Early Years Learning Framework (EYLF; Australian Government, Department of Education, Employment and Workplace Relations, 2009).

Link between play and the VEYLDF and EYLF

Within a construct of "Being, Belonging, and Becoming", five key learning and development outcomes for children are outlined including: (1) a strong sense of

Table 7.2 Linking the five learning outcomes (VEYDLF & EYLF) with pretend play skills on the Pretend Play Checklist for Teachers (Stagnitti & Paatsch, 2018)

Five learning outcomes (VEYDLF & EYLF)	Play scripts	Sequences of play actions	Object substitution	Figurine play	Role play
Identity	Emerging autonomy. Knowledgeable and confident self-identities.	Feel safe, secure, and supported. Emerging autonomy. Knowledgeable and confident self-identities.	Emotional understanding of self and of others.	Interact with empathy, care, and respect.	All sub-outcomes are covered in Role Play.
Communication	Interact verbally and non-verbally, engage with a range of texts, express ideas using a range of media with media considered as the ability to access, analyse, evaluate, and create information in various forms.	Express ideas using a range of media, understand symbols and patterns, using technologies to represent thinking, where technologies is considered here as the application of science or knowledge to practice (i.e., this can include imposing meaning or representations on objects and actions).	Interact verbally and non-verbally, engage with a range of texts, express ideas using a range of media, understand symbols and patterns, using technologies to represent thinking.	Interact verbally and non-verbally, engage with a range of texts, express ideas using a range of media – character monologue.	

Five learning outcomes (VEYDLF & EYLF)	Play scripts	Sequences of play actions	Object substitution	Figurine play	Role play
Learning	All sub-outcomes of learning.	Develop a range of dispositions for learning, curiosity, cooperation, confidence, creativity, commitment, imagination, perseverance. Range of skills, problem solving, hypothesizing, inquiry, research and investigation.	Develop a range of dispositions for learning, curiosity, cooperation, confidence, creativity, commitment, imagination, perseverance. Range of skills, problem solving, hypothesizing, inquiry, research and investigation.	Transfer and adapt what they have learnt. Resource through creating connections between, people, place, technologies and materials.	
Wellbeing	Take responsibility for their own health and wellbeing.	Strong in their social, emotional and spiritual wellbeing.	Strong in their social, emotional and spiritual wellbeing.	Strong in their social, emotional, and spiritual wellbeing. Take responsibility for their own health and wellbeing.	
Community	Sense of belonging.	Develop awareness of fairness, socially responsible.	Research identifies links to social cohesion.	Sense of belonging, respond to diversity.	

identity, (2) effective communicators, (3) confident and involved learners, (4) a strong sense of wellbeing, and (5) connection with, and contribution to, their world. In addition, each learning outcome includes guiding principles and practices. The VEYLDF and EYLF recognise an integrated approach to teaching practice including adult-led, child-led, and guided play.

Table 7.2 presents the links between the attributes of the five learning outcomes set out in the VEYLDF and pretend play skills. The five learning outcomes are presented in the first column, while the five pretend plays skills outlined in the PPCT (Stagnitti & Paatsch, 2018) are presented in the remaining columns.

Conclusion

There is a large body of research that has highlighted the link between play and the many areas of academic, cognitive, linguistic, and social and emotional development. In this chapter we have presented the ways in which play provides rich opportunities for children to achieve the described outcomes outlined in curriculum documents and learning frameworks, particularly the Australian Curriculum and the VEYLDF. Specifically, we have provided practical examples to support teachers to understand that play is a way of doing rather than an add on. We argue that through play teachers can observe, assess, and report on children's achievements across all leaning areas and outcomes, and general capabilities.

References

Australian Curriculum, Assessment and Reporting Authority (ACARA). (2020). Retrieved from https://www.australiancurriculum.edu.au/f-10-curriculum/.

Australian Government Department of Education, Employment and Workplace Relations (AG). (2009). *Belonging, being & becoming: The Early Years Learning Framework for Australia*. Canberra, ACT: DEEWR for the Council of Australian Governments.

Cavanaugh, D. M., Clemence, K. J., Teale, M. M., Rule, A. C., & Montgomery, S. E. (2017). Kindergarten scores, storytelling, executive function, and motivation improved through literacy-rich guided play. *Early Childhood Education Journal*, 45, 831–843. doi:10.1007/s10643-016-0832-8.

Creaghe, N., Quinn, S., & Kidd, E. (2021). Symbolic play provides a fertile context for language development. *Infancy*, 26(6), 980–1010. doi:10.1111.infa.12422.

Department of Education and Training, Victoria (2016). *Victorian Early Years Learning and Development Framework: For all children from birth to eight years*. Victorian Government, East Melbourne. Retrieved from https://www.vic.gov.au/victorian-early-years-learning-development-framework-veyldf.

Dockett, S., & Perry, B. (2010). What makes mathematics play? In *MERGA 33: Shaping the future of mathematics education* (pp. 715–718). Mathematics Education Research Group of Australasia.

Hirsh-Pasek, K., Golinkoff, R. M., Berk, L. E., & Singer, D. (2009). *A mandate for playful learning in preschool: Applying the scientific evidence*. Oxford University Press. doi:10.1093/acprof:oso/9780195382716.001.0001.

Hollenstein, L., Thurnheer, S., & Vogt, F. (2022). Problem solving and digital transformation: Acquiring skills through pretend play in kindergarten. *Education Sciences*, 12(2), 92. doi:10.3390/educsci12020092.

Holmes, R. M., Kohm, K., Genise, S., Koolidge, L., Mendelson, D., Romeo, L., & Bant, C. (2022). Is there a connection between children's language skills, creativity, and play? *Early Child Development and Care*, 192(8), 1178–1189. doi:10.1080/03004430.2020.1853115.

Jay, J. A., & Knaus, M. (2018). Embedding play-based learning into junior primary (Year 1 and 2) curriculum in WA. *Australian Journal of Teacher Education (Online)*, 43(1), 112–126.

Moedt, K., & Holmes, R. M. (2020). The effects of purposeful play after shared storybook readings on kindergarten children's reading comprehension, creativity, and language skills and abilities. *Early Child Development and Care*, 190(6), 839–854. doi:10.1080/03004430.2018.1496914.

Nolan, A., & Paatsch, L. (2018). (Re) affirming identities: Implementing a play-based approach to learning in the early years of schooling. *International Journal of Early Years Education*, 26(1), 42–55. doi:10.1080/09669760.2017.1369397.

Parker, R., Thomsen, B. S., & Berry, A. (2022, February). Learning through play at school: A framework for policy and practice. *Frontiers in Education*, 7, 751801. Frontiers Media SA. doi:10.3389/feduc.2022.751801.

Quinn, S., Donnelly, S., & Kidd, E. (2018). The relationship between symbolic play and language acquisition: A meta-analytic review. *Developmental Review*, 49, 121–135. doi:10.1016/j.dr.2018.05.005.

Stagnitti, K., & Paatsch, L. (2018). The pretend play checklist for teachers. Learn to Play. www.learntoplayevents.com.

Stagnitti, K. E., Paatsch, L., Nolan, A., & Campbell, K. (2020). Identifying play skills that predict children's language in the beginning of the first year of school. *Early Years*, 1–15. doi:10.1080/09575146.2020.1865280.

Victorian Curriculum and Assessment Authority (2017). *Victorian F–10 Curriculum*. VCAA, Melbourne.

Victorian Department of Education and Early Childhood Development (DEECD) & Victorian Curriculum and Assessment Authority (VCAA). (2009). *Victorian Early Years Learning and Development Framework for all children from birth to eight years*. East Melbourne: DEECD.

Wiggins, G., Wiggins, G. P., & McTighe, J. (2005). *Understanding by design*. ASCD.

Wilkinson, J. A. (2004). Rike's guided dramatic play systems, the brain, and language. In R. L. Clements & L. Fiorentino (Eds.), *The child's right to play: A global approach* (pp. 263–275). Praeger.

Wilkinson, J. A., & Rike, E. K. (1993). Guided symbolic dramatic play as the missing link to literacy. In J. A. Wilkinson (Ed.), *The symbolic dramatic play–literacy connection: Whole brain, whole body, holistic learning* (pp. 9–24). Ginn Press.

Worthington, M., & van Oers, B. (2016). Pretend play and the cultural foundations of mathematics. *European Early Childhood Education Research Journal*, 24(1), 51–66. doi:10.1080/1350293X.2015.1120520.

Yoon, H. S. (2014). Can I play with you? The intersection of play and writing in a kindergarten classroom. *Contemporary Issues in Early Childhood*, 15(2), 109–121.

8 How to Create a Play-based Approach to Learning

The authors of this book have supported government, Catholic, and private schools across various locations in Australia in implementing a guided pretend play approach to the curriculum. In our experience, every school has employed a different method in supporting the inclusion of play-based learning. This approach to learning is dependent on the culture and values of the school, knowledge of play within a school, and the presence of a "champion of play". In our experience, the "champion of play" draws on knowledge and understanding of play to guide other school staff in ensuring expectations related to curriculum outcomes are being addressed, aiming to enhance the long-term learning outcomes of students and pedagogical expertise.

Chapter 7 argued that play is not an add on, as it can be embedded within teaching practice, with strong links back to guidelines within the curriculum, to meet learning goals in a more accessible way for the student. Chapters 2–6 have explored the research and understanding of play, and the integral role pretend play holds in the whole development of the child, including learning, language, self-regulation, social competence, creativity, and storytelling. From here, Chapter 9 will outline the role of the teacher and Chapter 10 will explore how play can be assessed in school age children. This provides insight into how a school could identify the play strengths of children within a classroom. This knowledge informs teaching strategies and teachers can draw on that understanding to enhance learning through play at a classroom level and potentially within a whole school approach.

Understanding the value of play

The first step in implementing a play-based approach involves the school and/or teacher teams having a shared vision and understanding of play. The two primary guiding principles here are that:

1 Play, in this case pretend play, is understood and the principles underpinning play-based learning are valued.
2 Children learn best when they feel happy and safe. Engaging in joyful playful interactions is a positive gateway in supporting engagement in learning.

DOI: 10.4324/9781003296782-10

There is a strong focus on pretend play in this book because there is a large body of evidence supporting play-based learning in developing higher order thinking (HOT) capacities, alongside critical learning capacities for the 21st century learner. The latter being creativity, critical thinking, content, communication, collaboration, and confidence (Golinkoff & Hirsch-Pasek, 2016). Guided pretend play can also be implemented across indoor and outdoor settings within a school, and therefore provides flexibility to achieving student engagement.

Student engagement supports effective learning

Chapter 2 outlined the experience of daily interactions and the felt or perceived sense of safety on the developing brain and subsequent learning opportunities of a child. Bringing attention back to a quote provided in Chapter 2 helps to shape an understanding of the importance of teacher–student interactions. Activating children's social engagement system opens them to learning. As Haim Ginott (1972, p. 12) so astutely stated in relation to a teacher:

> It is my personal approach that creates the climate. It is my daily mood that makes the weather. I possess tremendous power to make a child's life miserable [*e.g., by invoking fear and punishment*] or joyous [*e.g., by being responsive, smiling, eye contact, calm rhythmic speaking*]. I can humiliate or humor, hurt or heal. My response decides whether a crisis will be escalated [*e.g., a child's flight or fight system is activated*] or de-escalated [*e.g., a child's social engagement system is activated*], and a child humanized or dehumanized.

For children to effectively engage in their learning, a perceived sense of safety must be felt. By understanding pretend play, the value of play, the underpinning principles in play-based learning, and reflecting on adult–teacher interactions within pedagogy, a large step is taken towards effectively engaging the learner. Guided play provides a powerful medium to achieve this. Research by Barker et al. (2014) highlighted that children who spent more time is less structured activities (that is, activities that promoted a creative licence and self-initiation), demonstrated better self-directed executive functions or self-regulatory capacity than those in a structured setting. An engaged learner will also experience a sense of joy in their interactions with learning and others in their space. Joy heightens motivation and interest in learning and is a necessary component for developing and integrating strong neural connections in the brain, supporting memory retrieval (Lee et al., 2023; see also Chapter 2).

A shared vision

To achieve a shared vision may involve taking a courageous leap. A shared vision involves establishing shared values and a mission statement prompting motivation for learning and growth for the school community, which could involve teacher, students, and the wider parent community. It can feel overwhelming, but starting with one or two classes is a start. This start must begin with an understanding of the two principles outlined above. By working through a shared vision process, five steps can be taken to support the sustainability of implementing a play-based approach. The first step involves understanding the purpose, that is, that play is valued as an effective medium to support children's learning. This is followed by the second step, which is a discussion around the current reality: what are the current tensions that may exist for teacher–student interactions, classroom behaviour, truancy, and learning outcomes in your school? The third step involves identifying strategies to move forward. This can be supported by accessing professional development, attending workshops on the implementation of play within schools, reading a wide variety of resources, and visiting schools who are at later stages of the journey (an example is given later in this chapter and in Chapter 11). The fourth step is to plan for involvement by all stakeholders (especially parents) and encourage open communication between students, teachers, and the wider school community. The fifth and final step is a commitment to the lived experience, identifying individual biases and motivations in the process of change (Stoner, 2023). These steps can be applied at the classroom and/or the whole school level.

Observing play and connecting play to skills

A rural school in Victoria adopted the approach of assessing all children's pretend play ability as they entered the foundation year, or first year of formal schooling. After two years of using this practice, the teachers commented that the information provided through the play assessment at the beginning of the year (early in Term 1) increased their understanding of the strengths of a student and how the student processed information. Without the play assessment, it would take teachers until Term 3 to naturally gather the same information. Creating efficiency in their understanding of the students' ability, this assessment process had a significant impact on the teacher's pedagogical approach to the first year of formal schooling, and subsequently the learning outcomes for the children.

Chapter 10 outlines various assessment tools in supporting an understanding of a child's play, interaction, or self-initiated pretend play ability within a classroom-based setting. Play assessment not only guides the setting of learning goals, but can inform teacher–child interactions. One of the assessments presented in Chapter 10 is the Pretend Play Checklist for Teachers (PPCT). This assessment is designed for use in a classroom and provides teachers with information on observing play across the five skills of pretend play: play scripts, sequences of play actions, object substitution, figurine play, and role play. This assessment can be used to assess individual students or a group of students. The information gathered provides a deeper understanding of the children's developing profile.

A description is provided here of the how the five play skills assessed using the PPCT can inform pedagogy and essentially efforts towards the interrelated suite of skills to support the 21st century learner (Collaboration, Communication, Content, Critical Thinking, Creative Innovation, and Confidence) (Golinkoff &

Hirsch-Pasek, 2016). Measuring a child's complexity of play scripts provides insight into their current understanding of their awareness of self and others. If children's play scripts remain within a domestic theme, this indicates a less complex understanding of the world around them, impacting on their ability to collaborate with others. If children's play scripts have extended to the fantasy level, this is an indication that they are absorbing ideas and exploring concepts from literature and screen, and starting to extend their thinking beyond reality or everyday experience. They are demonstrating a capacity for creative and critical thinking, exploring content that brings confidence in their developing self-representation.

By observing children's complexity in their sequences of play, an insight into their logical sequential thinking is achieved. If children are playing out four to five pretend play actions in a repetitive manner, this provides insight into a less complex organisation of thinking ability in comparison to a child's play that consists of sub plots, problems embedded throughout the play, a narrative that can extend potentially over hours verses minutes. This has implications for children's narrative and literacy development and provides insight into their language acquisition, self-regulatory capacity, and higher order thinking. More complex use of sequences of play actions extends the opportunity to communicate with others in a collaborative way as more complex content is explored in interactions.

Observing the complexity of a child's ability to substitute objects as something else in the play provides an insight into their abstract thinking. As noted previously in Chapter 6, the ability to use objects and represent them as something else supports the capacity for creativity, divergent thinking, problem solving, counter-factual thinking, and flexibility in their thinking. If a child remains at the less complex level of using objects for their functional purpose, flexibility in thinking can be impacted. The child presents as less playful and therefore opportunities to engage with others in play is reduced. If a teacher's observations noted that a student can pick up any object, describe its function, impose attributes, turn that object into something else as the story line changes, then further observations may also note: flexibility in their thinking as opposed to rigidity, the increased use of language, the increase in the student's ability to grasp concepts relating to maths (for example, comparing weight, size, sounds, and relationships between objects such as balancing), narrative, self-regulation, and social competence. These observations support all areas of the six C's required for the 21st century learner.

Figurine play provides insight into the child's ability to decentre play away from themselves and impose meaning on another. If a figurine is viewed as an object in play, as opposed to a character that might come alive, this has implications for children's developing theory of mind. When a figurine comes "alive" in the play, the child starts to do things with the figurine, and consideration is given to developing characterisation. For example, What might that character be thinking?, What motivates this character?, How does the character speak and What is the emotion that is expressed through the character to support the narrative?. Characterisation in play provides children with the opportunity to develop an understanding that others can think differently, and interactions can have different influences on the developing story line or narrative in the play. To decentre the play away from oneself requires the capacity to demonstrate creativity with confidence, feeding into the capacity for social competence, and supporting the opportunity for collaboration with peers in a more complex communicative pattern.

Role play provides children with an opportunity to develop cultural awareness, a wider understanding of their world around them. This requires the capacity for critical thinking and communication. What are the roles they see in society and how do they make sense of those? Observations might indicate that a child is still at the level of complexity of observing and imitating others in their play, suggesting they are still processing an understanding of others within their immediate social world. Other children might be taking on the role of an astronaut and exploring all the complexities of language, motivation, resources needed, and considerations for how an astronaut might interact with others. This skill provides opportunities for children to further develop emotional understanding and self-regulation capacity as outlined in Chapter 4. When role play is placed within a shared narrative with others the skill of collaboration with confidence can develop (see Chapter 5).

The above has outlined how an understanding of play can be achieved through play assessment, supporting an understanding of a child's developing profile and resulting in a strengths-based approach to inform learning goals associated with literacy development, critical and creative thinking, math concepts and executive functioning, attention to task, problem solving, speaking, and listening and the six C's of the 21st century learner. In Box 8.1 a vignette is presented of how one school has used the Pretend Play Checklist for Teachers (PPCT) to inform their teaching strategies for Foundation children.

Box 8.1 A Foundation classroom and the Pretend Play Checklist for Teachers
By Jacqui Jarvis and Peter Fahey

At the beginning of each year considerable attention is given to the design and layout of the Foundation classroom. Play opportunities are both visible and accessible to the children. Initially opportunities are based on known experiences including the home corner, shops or a doctor's clinic. The children are familiar with the experiences using their personal play scripts, for example, Figure 8.1 shows a home corner play scene.

Mini-worlds (see Figure 8.2) also occupy the space with a mixture of conventional and symbolic play pieces such as doll houses, farms, dinosaurs, figurines and sticks. Educators spend the first few weeks both attuning and tracking alongside the children in their play. This important time builds relationships and trust with the children. Children who have play difficulties are noticeable often displaying poor language skills, comprehension, and story sequencing.

During the first few weeks all Foundation children are filmed in mixed gender groups of 3–4 over 3 observation sessions using the PPCT (Pretend

Figure 8.1 A home corner play scene for Foundation children. Photograph by Jacqui Jarvis. Used with permission.

Figure 8.2 A mini world of a farm used in Foundation class. Photograph by Jacqui Jarvis. Used with permission.

Play Checklist for Teachers) as a guide. Play scenarios are set up by the educators in a quiet learning space using play pieces in mini worlds and prepared pretend play scenarios. The educators analyse the results using the PPCT. The PPCT enables the teachers to provide scaffolded intervention at the point of need. These skills are not identified with current early years assessments such as the Observation Survey. This important information informs modelled and guided play future sessions.

Within the Foundation classroom, teachers align instruction with the Victorian Curriculum. Therefore, there is regular literacy and numeracy instruction alongside play-based learning.

Over time updated observational data from the PPCT is used to rearrange current play scenarios adding in new figures or props or build in new learning centres such as a vet clinic or hospital. The environment continues to change reflecting the evolving skills and learning characteristics of the children. Conventional play pieces are exchanged for symbolic play pieces and more unknown pretend play experiences such as going on a plane or going to the hairdresser allow for more involved play. Mini world and role play are used throughout the year to support social and emotional development. For example, often after lunch and recess, modelled play about an incident is needed. Children watch the adults model scenarios and then collaborate, with guided support in small groups to play out the appropriate solutions.

Planning a guided pretend play approach

The beginning stages of implementing play-based learning can take time. Depending on the understanding and value of play within the school setting, this may take years. Planning involves several considerations, such as, the school's values and culture, the understanding of play within a child's wellbeing and development, the physical resources of a school, the physical space of a school, the support of the parent and general community, and the commitment of teachers and leadership of the school. As well as this, each school needs to consider how much time within the day to devote to embedding play and how to structure this time.

Implementing play within the classroom – examples from schools across Australia

Following the identification of play as an approach to inform pedagogy, schools have created and developed different methods in implementing play-based learning in the classroom. The method adopted by schools is dependent on the considerations outlined above and the school's unique journey, honouring the understanding that play is complex and the benefits of such a learning approach are wide. An example is now given of a school who started the journey of implementing play-based learning within the classroom. This school also used the Pretend Play Checklist for Teachers (PPCT– see Chapter 10) to inform teaching strategies. Assessment supported the developing understanding of children's strengths in their play. This informed the teacher on how to pitch the introduction of the skills of pretend play to the class. The teacher would present one play skill per week, spending 20 minutes demonstrating the skill in a variety of narratives. This was then followed by 40 minutes of guided play where the children were practicing the skill. As children played and interacted throughout the week, the teacher explicitly noted and highlighted the skill when she saw it in joyful interactions in the class and outdoor settings. The teacher would then embed the skill throughout the curriculum to support learning outcomes through the play. For example, if the focus skill was role play, she would choose students to take on roles and act out a story as she read it. If the pretend play skill focus for the week was figurine play, she would use a puppet character to read a story or select students to retell a story with miniatures, such as small characters within created play scenes.

Another school found they had limited space and time. Following assessment of the children's play, it became apparent there was a significant gap in children's use of unstructured objects in play, that is, their ability to use objects and substitute them as something else, which has implications for the children's developing creativity, problem, solving, flexibility in their thinking, counterfactual thinking, self- regulation, social connectedness, language development, understanding of maths concepts, and generalised learning capabilities. The school decided to dedicate one hour per day, using the classroom floor space to explore the use of unstructured objects (i.e., boxes, cloth, sticks, pebbles and general loose parts) in a guided way for play. Due to the limited space, the classroom floor was used and items were packed away following the session. The classroom teacher used a guided play approach.

Another school in Victoria dedicated two hour blocks, four mornings a week, where three year levels (Foundation/1/2), could come together and explore different play stations. This school had a large centralised dedicated space designed to support multi-age play development. The teaching team underwent training prior to the implementation of this program early in the school year. Within the training there were teachers who were apprehensive about play-based learning. Six months after the implementation of play-based learning, one of the apprehensive teachers greeted Karen Stagnitti and Louise Paatsch and said, "You must come and have a look at what they are doing. I wouldn't have believed it".

Play-based learning requires a level of commitment. Initially the spaces can be noisy and appear chaotic and disorganised. At this point, often the process of implementing play is abandoned. The authors encourage schools to remain committed. With guided support the children begin to calm, self-regulate, and demonstrate a higher level of organisation in their storytelling. This can take from one to six months. Students begin to engage in a collective social manner and memory retrieval for past play interactions and storytelling.

Another school located within Victoria used a combination of these approaches to support their students. All students entering the first year of formal schooling participated in a pretend play assessment and shared with Siobhan Casey their strengths in play skills. Assessment had identified that children across the classes were experiencing challenges below their expected range for age, for object use and storytelling. With limited resources, a play storytelling approach was implemented once per week for each year level from Foundation through to Year 2. (An expanded version of this example is presented in Chapter 6.) Within this approach primarily unstructured objects were used. Following the modelling of a narrative using the objects, children were encouraged to play and pretend the objects were something else, by giving the objects properties (i.e., fast car), by describing invisible elements (reference to absent objects) and embedding these ideas in the development of their story. Opportunities were given for more complex players to extend, and less complex players to feel safe with a basic structure.

Another school implemented a one-hour investigation time slot at the end of each day in Foundation year. Play assessment was used to inform teacher–student interactions in the "investigations" time at the end of the day. Teachers and support staff guided the investigations. Following this experience of play-based learning, teachers commented on their own shift in their thinking on play and their understanding about how and when skills are acquired.

Resources for play-based learning within the classroom

Guided play informs pedagogy in a play-based setting. Resources exist both online and throughout this book to support the implementation of play activities within the classroom. Table 8.1 presents a list of resources suggested as a starting point for play scenarios.

Resources need to include a collection of both toys and unstructured objects (see Table 8.1). Unstructured play materials can include large and small cardboard boxes, recycled paper/newspaper, fabric, cardboard tubes, recycled cartons, natural play materials such as twigs, leaves, seed pods, pebbles. For ideas on using unstructured objects, a free resource to download is *Pretending with Objects*, available at https://www.learntoplayevents.com/product/pretending-with-objects/.

These resources can be utilised to set up a round robin style play scenario. To support children to develop play skills, schools have grouped children in no more than four children per group. This allowed for a teacher, learning support officer, and one more support staff to float around the room guiding and scaffolding the play where appropriate. Enough toy/object resources are required to be spread across the group; for example, figurine play resources would need enough figurines for each student in the group. For a whole of class or cohort round robin approach, stations can include resources for play and curriculum goals at each station (also see Chapter 9 for the role of the teacher).

A model of best practice

St James Parish Primary School in regional Victoria, Australia, is considered a model of best practice in the implementation of play-based learning at the whole school level. Their journey began in 2005 and continues through to current times.

Table 8.1 Suggested list of resources to begin play-based learning, guided by the Pretend Play Checklist for Teachers

Play Scene	Resources	Play opportunities and skills
Home Cooking Corner Can evolve into restaurant play/café	Stainless steel cookware, wooden kitchen Dolls of differing cultural backgrounds Girls Boys Tea set Chef role play set	Role play – understanding language, behaviour, and context of roles. In a social context – cooperating, negotiating, problem solving. Supporting narrative – including forward thinking, planning, cause and effect, carrying out play scenario over 2–3 days – development of logical sequential thinking.
Shopping Scene	Coles mini's Cash register Shopping bags Larger grocery items Boxes for Eftpos cards/ machine	As above
Farm Scene	All resources available for farm scene – include non-structured items such as felt, boxes, stones, sticks, and tea towels. Flexible dolls. Farm animals that stand. Fences that stand.	Character play – creating a small play scene with characters.
Cubby Scene – can evolve into treasure island, volcano play	Blankets Play silks Cushions	Play scripts – stories can reflect anything and can include cause and effect.
Tubs – Pirate Theme Space Theme Queens/Kings/Dragons Treasure Island	Small toy sets that reflect the themes as well as unstructured objects	As above
Doctors	Doctor set Teddys/doll/figurines	Play stories – stories reflect less frequent life events.
Hairdressers	Hairdressing kit	Play stories – stories reflect less frequent life events.
Dolls House	Dolls furniture kit Unstructured materials/loose parts	The use of more complex toys with characters – understanding wider context.
Construction Play	Outdoor wooden construction set, 12 pieces. Natural spaces STEM kit, 112 pieces. Complete set of 4 hats.	Object substitution – can construct using many objects to create a new object.

In 2023, the pedagogy in the school keeps being refined and developed. In 2022 the National Assessment Program for Literacy and Numeracy (NAPLAN) data for the school showed reading with an average growth at 138.4 points compared to the Australian average at 70.6 points (personal communication with Peter Fahey, co-principal, St James Parish School). Staff engagement was at the 99th percentile and student engagement, behaviour, peer relations, and community engagement verged close to or above the 90th percentiles (personal communication with Peter Fahey, co-principal St James Parish School). Here is a link to view the overall current approach to pedagogy at St James: https://youtu.be/SscOuyHLjnI

Creating a shared vision

St James called this a "passion for possibilities!" The staff as a collective believed they had the power and ability to make a real difference to lives of the students in their care. They established a collective commitment to bring about positive change, identifying the need for "a metamorphosis of education – from the cocoon, a butterfly should emerge. Improvement does not give us a butterfly, only a faster caterpillar" (Stagnitti et al., 2013, p. 93). A number of confronting, uncomfortable, and challenging questions were asked, as a collective, shared vision for change was identified. Through research, deep questioning, and visiting other progressive schools, St James deepened their understanding of what children needed to thrive at school. This led to a significant change in the teachers' fundamental paradigms about the role of education and pedagogy (Stagnitti et al., 2013).

The school set out to honestly describe their current reality. In 2005 they were experiencing a lack of student engagement, and children with significant behavioural issues and low academic performance. The children's oral language ability was low, high incidences of anti-social aggressive behaviour were observed, and there were serious doubts as to whether the current pedagogy was effective. Strategies and actions to move forward were explored.

By 2008 significant educational change had started to emerge. At this point the school engaged with Karen Stagnitti to begin the process of understanding and implementing play within the curriculum, and by 2009 improvements in children's oral language, social connectedness, and complexity in play were identified (Reynolds et al., 2011). By 2011 a new strategic plan had been adopted and reviewed.

This process resulted in a shift from a traditional classroom with tables and chairs and a timetable, to a play-based approach. The teacher's role undertook a shift to become a facilitator of learning. Staff and students adopted six key focus words – imagination, diversity, expression, relationships, reflection, and discovery. All staff needed to have a common understanding of, and commitment to, a contemporary philosophy of learning and teaching. This philosophy embraced children as strong, capable and competent, curious and creative beings. Building on children's existing conceptual understandings (a constructivist approach) became the focus, and like-minded teachers, passionate about children and supporting their learning in this way, were necessary.

The following outcomes were observed by the school leadership following the implementation of the whole school approach in the early stages from 2005 to 2011.

- Children at the school communicated feeling nurtured, valued and respected.
- Teachers were described by their principal (Lynch, 2011) as being more passionate, motivated and committed to their roles, which were valued as critically important to student learning.
- The emotionally supportive environment built trust and respect, and behavioural concerns became minor and infrequent (Lynch, 2011).
- Insight SRC data on students' sense of wellbeing indicated a rise to approximately the 80th percentile in 2011, and student misbehaviour dropped to around the 20th percentile.
- Lynch (2011) observed that, following the changes, previously disengaged students were now highly motivated, actively engaged learners.
- Skill development and knowledge acquisition progressed more rapidly in a wide range of areas, not only relevant to the traditional subjects, but also problem solving skills, use of initiative and imagination, teamwork, creativity and interpersonal skills with "genuine collaboration" (Lynch, 2011).
- Wider community observations reflected a greater commitment by students to their social community (Stagnitti et al., 2013).
- There was an explicit respect for each other and each other's tools (e.g., pencils, rulers, scissors), with children looking after equipment and returning equipment for others.
- There was a decrease in truancy, and an increase in engagement throughout the school, with parents coming into the school to talk to teachers.
- Children understood and respected social cues and social contexts. For example, they would walk quietly around a conversation taking place in a circle, rather than loudly through it, as they had done in the past (Stagnitti et al., 2013).

Key tenets were established and continue to guide the personal commitment now shown by the staff to sustain and maintain the transformative approach. The key tenets involved the following (Stagnitti et al., 2013, p. 97):

- A child assimilates new understanding into an already existing framework.
- Children develop higher order cognitive thinking by engaging with the collective.
- To develop competence, children must have a foundation of factual knowledge and understand this in the light of a conceptual/theoretical framework.
- Children need to be able to self-regulate their learning. This "meta-cognitive" approach (i.e., thinking about thinking) enables children to realise their natural disposition and modulate it with scaffolded support. So, children need to be encouraged to think through how, what, and why they are learning.

The above tenets form the underpinning principles of play-based learning.

Conclusion

Planning the implementation of a play-based pedagogy requires a team-based collective approach. The understanding of the value of play and the belief that children learn best when they feel safe and experience joyful interactions with others is central to developing a shared vision. The journey towards the shared vision is unique to every school and depends on a variety of precipitating factors. Models of best practice do exist. There is a community of schools who are at the beginning of the journey, and with careful consideration, are finding effective ways of implementing a play-based pedagogy, whilst at the same time enhancing teacher satisfaction and creating change for the long-term learning outcomes of their students. Supports do exist for schools wanting to take the leap, and the authors encourage those who wish to consider such a leap to remain committed, as the outcomes will come with time.

References

Barker, J. E., Semenov, A. D., Michaelson, L., Provan, L. S., Snyder, H. R., & Munakata, Y. (2014). Less-structured time in children's daily lives predicts self-directed executive functioning. *Frontiers in Psychology*, 5, 593. doi:10.3389/fpsyg.2014.00593.

Ginott, H. (1972). *Teacher and child: A book for parents and teachers.* Macmillan.

Golinkoff, R. M., & Hirsch-Pasek, K. (2016). *Becoming brilliant: What science tells us about raising successful children.* American Psychological Association.

Lee, J., Lee, H., Masters, A. Fletcher, K., Suh, D., Golinkoff, R., & Hirsh-Pasek, K. (2023). Bringing playful learning to South Korea: An alternative pedagogical approach to promote children's learning and success. *International Journal of Educational Development*, 97. doi:10.1016/j.iedudev.2022.102710.

Lynch, B. (2011). At the chalkface: Transforming education. *Teacher* journal archive, 2011 (222). https://research.acer.edu.au/teacher/vol2011/iss222/18/.

Reynolds, E., Stagnitti, K., & Kidd, E. (2011). Play, language and social skills of children attending a play-based curriculum school and a traditionally structured classroom curriculum school in low socioeconomic areas. *Australasian Journal of Early Childhood*, 4, 120. doi:10.1177/183693911103600416.

Stagnitti, K., Frawley, M., Lynch, B., & Fahey, P. (2013). Increasing social cohesiveness in a school environment. In A. Taket, B. Crisp, M. Graham, L. Hanna, S. Goldinay & L. Wilson (Eds.), *Practising social inclusion* (pp. 91–105). Routledge.

Stoner, J. L. (2023, 10 February). How to create a shared vision that works. Retrieved from https://seapointcenter.com/how-to-create-a-shared-vision/.

9 The Role of the Teacher in Supporting Children's Play

Research has shown that the teacher's role in children's play covers a broad spectrum of roles from guiding or being a player in the child's play to that of being an observer, with a more facilitative "hands off" approach (Beecher & Arthur, 2001; Danniels & Pyle, 2023; Pyle & Danniels, 2017; Weisberg et al., 2016; Zosh et al., 2018). For some teachers, embedding play into the classroom creates a different role that may disrupt their typical practices and may lead to changes in the ways that they set up their classroom, how they may interact with the children, and how they understand what learning takes place across all areas of the curriculum within the play context. For example, in some of our recent engagement with teachers as we worked together to embed a play-based approach in their classrooms, many reported their uncertainties regarding their role. As two teachers stated:

> I often struggle with what is the teacher's role in that pretend play. When do I step in and when is the right time?
>
> (Alistair, Foundation teacher)

> I guess if we build on first what our role is [during children's play in the classroom], what should we be doing during this time, before going onto the assessment, before going on to written observations?
>
> (Hannah, Year 1 teacher)

This chapter discusses the critical role that teachers play in supporting children's learning within the play context. Specifically, we propose the importance of guided play and the various roles that teachers perform during the children's play. We also highlight the specific teaching strategies that may be implemented as part of these roles, including scaffolding, setting up the classroom environment for play, facilitating, modelling, and demonstrating. Vignettes and practical examples are provided throughout the chapter to illustrate these teacher roles and strategies, and the ways in which they scaffold children's play and learning.

DOI: 10.4324/9781003296782-11

Guided play: scaffolding children's learning

As discussed previously throughout this book, Vygotsky's (1967; 1978) socio-cultural approach focusses on the importance of socialisation and the active role of interaction between the child and adults in supporting children's learning. We have also highlighted that play is a socially meaningful activity and is a rich context in which important concepts and social skills can be created, discovered, and mastered (Creaghe, 2020). Play is pleasurable, social, iterative, and involves active "minds on" thinking (Danniels & Pyle, 2023; Zosh et al., 2018). Researchers often argue that play is a vehicle for children's learning and is important to children's academic, intellectual, social, and emotional development (Nolan & Paatsch, 2018; Stagnitti et al., 2000; Zosh et al., 2018).

Vygotsky's theory also posits that play is a zone of proximal development (ZPD) whereby competent players and language users (including teachers, parents, caregivers, or more competent peers) scaffold children to reach their next level of learning and development. The ZPD is central in understanding the importance of social relations for children's development (Hedegaard, 2012). Scaffolding requires the adult to undertake a variety of roles that depend on understandings of the child's current level of development and the ways to implement a range of strategies to support the child to move to the next level. As such, the role of the teacher during children's play becomes of paramount importance in supporting children's play and learning.

Research suggests that there are diverse viewpoints around the role of the adult in supporting children's play (Beecher & Arthur, 2001; Hedegaard, 2012; Pyle & Danniels, 2017; Weisberg et al., 2013; Utami et al., 2022). Some researchers suggest that teachers should only provide children with unstructured time to explore so that they do not hinder the child's play, also reporting that some teachers are reluctant to join in the play in case they take over (Beecher & Arthur, 2001; Jones & Reynolds, 1992). This child-directed and voluntary play without teacher involvement is often referred to as "free play". In contrast, other researchers highlight the importance of teacher's involvement in children's play as they prepare the environment and scaffold the child to reach the intended learning goal (Christie & Enz, 1992; Hedegaard, 2012; Weisberg et al., 2013; Utami et al., 2022). Zosh et al. (2018) acknowledge these diverse views and propose the need to develop a more multidimensional definition of play. They suggest that there is a "spectrum of play opportunities from free play through guided play to games and then playful direct instruction (a form of direct instruction with minor playful elements to try to keep children engaged)" (p. 9).

Similarly, Weisberg et al. (2016) advocate that there needs to be a middle ground between children participating in free play and teacher-directed play, suggesting the use of "guided play". Guided play combines child-directed learning experiences in free play with adult "mentorship" and a focus on learning outcomes (p. 177). Specifically, Weisberg and colleagues propose two forms of guided play:

1   *Designing the classroom environment to support a learning goal* but ensuring that the children have autonomy and agency to explore and lead within this environment. For example, the teacher may set up a fruit and vegetable shop play scene to promote children's mathematical learning of money and mass, narrative development, and vocabulary knowledge to include names of fruit and vegetables.

2   *Observing child-directed activities and scaffolding.* This involves watching and listening to children and contributing to their play by encouraging children to ask questions or prompting them to extend aspects of their play. For example, let's return to the fruit and vegetable shop. In this context, the teacher may support the learning of new vocabulary by asking the child what it is, or may present the fruit to the child and provide a label and description. The teacher may also observe the children in the play and note that there is no problem within the play script as they build their narrative. As such, the teacher may introduce a problem by stating that they forgot to bring their shopping basket to encourage the children to resolve the problem and to extend the play script.

In both these forms of play the teacher is showing sensitivity to children's ZPD by supporting their learning and encouraging engagement with the activities. At the same time, the child remains an agent of their own learning while the teacher can assess whether the child accomplished the learning goal.

There is a large body of research that has shown the significant benefits of guided play and the important role that teachers play. Weisberg et al. (2016) emphasized that "guided play leaves the locus of control with the child, allowing for self-directed exploration while enhancing learning and genuine enjoyment" (p. 178). They also suggest that guided play provides an excellent pedagogy that respects children's agency, develops children's love of learning, and supports a more "positive attitude toward learning itself" (p. 179). In an earlier study Weisberg et al. (2013) argued that guided play is a strong curricular approach to implementing academic content that is more child-centred and more developmentally appropriate when compared with more direct teaching approaches.

In a more recent study, Skene et al. (2022) conducted a systematic review and meta-analysis of 39 studies to compare guided play with free play in supporting children's learning and development. Findings showed that guided play has a greater positive effect on children's early maths and related skills such as spatial vocabulary, task switching, and knowledge of shapes, when compared with free play. In an earlier study by Sobel and Sommerville (2010) results showed that four-year-old children in a guided play environment were more accurate at learning causal relationships using their own exploratory actions that were supported by the adults than from direct instruction. Specifically, children first explored the toy that required the button to be pushed to turn on the light then received scaffolding from the adults (Sobel & Sommerville, 2010). Such interactions were more supportive than those where the adults told the child how the toy worked. Similar findings regarding the importance of adults in the play in supporting children's learning were reported in another recent study by Veresov et al. (2021)

that sought to explore whether children aged 5–6 years needed educator's support to develop their executive function (e.g., working memory and cognitive flexibility). The study included four types of adult intervention ranging from no involvement (free play), child-led with adult guidance (guided play) to entire organisation of the play (teacher-directed). Findings showed that during child-led play where an adult scaffolded the children by assigning roles or inventing a plot or acting out a play script with the child, children demonstrated greater progress in development than when there was no adult involvement or under complete adult direction. Gmitrová and Gmitrov (2003) also reported the strong link between teachers' involvement in pretend play and children's cognitive competence. Specially, they found that when teachers gently entered the children's play and provided opportunities for children to interact with their peers, children's cognitive and emotional development were supported (Gmitrová & Gmitrov, 2003). Together, these findings suggest that the role of the adult is critical in demonstrating, modelling, and supporting children to practice and develop particular executive functions, strengthening the argument for the importance of play in children's development.

It is well documented in the literature that teachers play an important role in supporting children's narrative and maths skills during play. For example, Utami et al. (2022) explored 38 4- to 5-year-old children's participation in a Playworld education intervention. Findings showed that the teachers engaged in an alternative pedagogical approach to formal learning by creating social situations within the narrative and presenting problems within the story. The teachers were less instructive and changed their strategies for delivering the learning content. They were emotionally engaged as a player in the scene, used the story scene as a way of supporting children's maths skills (counting and classification), and followed up on children's responses as they became involved in the play (Utami et al., 2022). The students engaged in imaginative play and co-constructed the story with the teacher, but were also provided opportunities to lead the play and be agents of their own learning. Similar benefits in supporting children's narrative during play were reported in a recent study by Brandisauskiene and Bredikyte (2022) that examined 113 teachers' practices in supporting aspects of narrative development such as settings, characters, plots, problem/s or story dilemmas, and resolutions. Findings from this qualitative study showed that the role of the teacher in the children's narrative development is crucial, as their actions determine the level of children's motivation, engagement, and opportunities to engage in the play and build story. Similarly, Hakkarainen et al. (2013) found that the adult's role in co-constructing the narrative with the children moved the children's narrative to a more complex level. They reported that the children were emotionally involved as the teachers helped to incorporate children's ideas into the story, highlighting the importance of adult–child interactions throughout the joint activity.

Together, these results illustrate the many varied viewpoints regarding defining play and the roles that teachers undertake as they support children in their play. Each role involves the implementation of a range of teaching strategies that differ according to the context of the play and the children's current level of understandings. In the following sections of this chapter, we present a framework for supporting teachers' understandings of the various roles and strategies that they may implement in supporting children's play and learning. Specifically, we have drawn on the work of Beecher and Arthur (2001) and Zosh et al. (2018).

Role of teacher: an integrated framework

Beecher and Arthur (2001) proposed a continuum of teaching strategies that incorporate the diverse roles that teachers undertake when involved in children's literacy-related play. The continuum acknowledges that the teacher's role will vary according to children's levels of ability and understanding. For example, there will be times when teachers will need to guide the children's play, while in other contexts the teacher will provide less support. Specifically, the continuum is presented as a straight line with four distinct roles: (1) onlooker, (2) stage manager, (3) co-player, and (4) play leader, demonstrating the changing levels of teacher support from less to more involvement. In addition, the continuum presents a series of indirect (e.g., modelling and acknowledging), mediating (e.g., scaffolding and co-constructing) and direct (e.g., demonstrating and providing explicit directions) teaching strategies that align to the various roles. We argue that these roles and strategies are not linear but rather are more interconnected and complementary as teachers move in and out of these roles within the same play activities.

Zosh et al. (2018) also present a linear representation of play as a six-point spectrum from free play to direct instruction. Each point is also described in relation to who initiates, who directs, and whether there is an explicit learning goal. The six points include: (1) free play that includes no involvement by the adult and where the child directs and initiates the play; (2) guided play where the play is initiated by the adult but directed by the child with adult involvement around a specific learning goal (this adult involvement may take the form of prompting or scaffolding the children, or setting up resources, space, or activity); (3) games that have a learning goal involving adult initiated and child directed; (4) co-opted play that is child-initiated and adult led with an explicit learning goal; (5) playful instruction which is a form of direct instruction that includes some playful elements that aim to engage the children; and (6) direct instruction where the adult initiates and directs the play. Again, we argue that teachers may undertake a number of these roles during children's play depending on the child's abilities and level of support required. We also posit that these roles are not represented in a linear way, but rather should be integrated and interconnected.

Figure 9.1 presents a framework that we have developed to demonstrate the interconnectedness between teacher roles, types of play, and teaching strategies that has been adapted from the work of Beecher and Arthur (2001) and Zosh et al. (2018). The four roles outlined by Beecher and Arthur (2001) are presented in the centre of the framework. Each role is then aligned to the type of play as outlined in Zosh et al. (2018) and some suggested teaching strategies that could be implemented by the teacher to support the child's play and learning. For

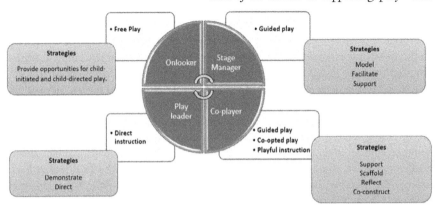

Figure 9.1 Framework of teacher roles and teaching strategies within different types of play

example, in the role of "Stage Manager", teachers may guide children's play through teaching strategies such as modelling, facilitating, and supporting particular skills. Facilitating the play may involve providing resources and experiences such as setting up a series of play spaces in the classroom including a café, a doctor's clinic, or an art gallery. Modelling may involve the teacher showing the children how a block could be used as a phone to tap for payment of their food at a café. In this example, the teacher models the play skill of object substitution and supports digital play. The teacher may also suggest that a child use the paper and pencil or a pretend iPad to take the order – an example of modelling literacy and digital play skills. Supporting children in the play may involve teachers giving assistance, acknowledging children's contributions, or may involve encouraging other children to become involved. For example, some children may observe the play and may not have sophisticated pragmatics skills to be able to initiate a conversation with their peers or know ways in which to enter a group. In such situations, the teacher may combine a number of teaching strategies, such as support and modelling of the verbal and non-verbal ways to initiate, to guide the child to enter the play.

It is important to note that a teacher may engage in several roles within a play activity that may involve the use of multiple teaching strategies. The play activity may also involve several play types. This framework highlights the critical role of the teacher in providing high levels of pedagogical expertise to create and support authentic and flexible play spaces that support all children's learning and development.

The following vignettes present various illustrative examples of the ways in which this framework can be applied to practice. Both vignettes are drawn from the practices of two teachers – Belinda and Rosanna. The school, located in a low socio-economic area, has implemented a play-based approach across the whole school for more than ten years. Currently the school is introducing more digital play into their classrooms, with the use of structured (e.g., toy phones, iPads, QR codes) and abstract (e.g., blocks for phones and bPay) objects.

Vignette 1

Belinda is a graduate teacher in her second year of teaching Foundation children. In the following example, Belinda implements several roles and teaching strategies. She also provides many opportunities for different play types throughout the session. Prior to the commencement of the session, Belinda set up several play scenes, "play stations", around the classroom. In one section of the room, she has set up a supermarket with toy groceries, electronic scanner, and food trollies. She has also set up some supermarket catalogues at a table with a QR code to check in. Another station is set up as a café, while another is set up with a table, sticks, feathers, pebbles, two magnifying glasses, and a white coat. The final area is located on the floor with a mat and some concrete (e.g., animals, bus, cars) and abstract, unstructured objects (e.g., pieces of material, sticks, pebbles, and blocks) that resemble paddocks for the animals, grass, and dirt (see Figure 9.2). At this stage, Belinda has facilitated the play by providing opportunities for child-initiated and child-directed play (free play) but may also encourage guided or direct-instruction play.

The children entered the classroom and explored the play stations, with all children selecting an area to play in. At first, Belinda observed the children (onlooker) at the stations. She then moved to the floor where four children were playing with the animals, blocks, and materials (see Figure 9.2). One child, Thomas, was manipulating and exploring all the objects, picking them up and putting them down. He was also observing the other children. At the same time, another child, Clara, had picked up the brown horse and pretended that the horse was eating the grass, making eating and neighing noises. Clara then moved the brown horse to join the other horses in the next paddock and the horses begin to talk to each other. The horses then moved towards the sheep and together the animals talked and raised the problem that there was no water to drink. Clara then picked up the white horse stating that "I will find some water for us to drink" and moved the horse to the blue piece of fabric and then returned it to the paddock.

Figure 9.2 Play scene set up by the teacher. Photograph by Louise Paatsch.

Belinda observed the two children (onlooker) but also gently acknowledged both children by smiling and nodding (stage manager who uses supporting teaching strategies). She then moved towards Thomas and began to label some of the animals he had picked up (a cow and koala) and says to Thomas that the animals are playing in the dirt (the brown material) and are hungry. Belinda then models eating actions and noises and Thomas begins to imitate. Belinda then picks up the koala and says "hello" to the cow. Thomas picks up the cow and says "hello, I'm hungry". He then starts to move the animals towards the paddock. In this segment of the play Belinda is guiding the play and moves between the roles of stage manager, play leader, and co-player, implementing the teaching strategies of scaffolding, modelling, and co-construction. As a result, Thomas is encouraged to move beyond object manipulation to the beginnings of developing a play script.

In the next part of the session, Belinda then moves to Clara, listens to her story then starts to join in the play by picking up the block and pretending it is a farmer. She quietly moves the farmer to the empty paddock and says "Oh no, where are my horses?" This exclamation results in Clara hiding the horses behind some sticks. Clara then picks up the farmer and goes to look for the horses and brings them back to the paddock. Belinda is no longer part of the play but continues to observe. Clara then picks up the horses and pretends to eat the grass. The horses then talk to each other saying "thank goodness I am back here", and "I like the farmer, I will take him for a ride". Clara then picks up the farmer and puts it on the horse's back. During this segment of the play, Belinda moves through all four roles and uses many teaching strategies to support Clara to extend her narrative. She observed, guided, and became a co-player and play leader throughout, and made choices as to when to initiate and direct, and when to allow Clara agency within the play.

Vignette 1 demonstrates the teacher's sensitivity to the children's levels of play and learning, and her pedagogical expertise in scaffolding both children to the next level of their development. Belinda used indirect strategies in the role of onlooker by encouraging both children to explore and experiment. She also used mediating and direct teaching strategies as co-player and play leader to support children's pretend play skills such as play scripts (e.g., a fictional story with the animals, and introducing a problem into the story), sequences of play action, and object substitution (e.g., using a block as a farmer). Belinda also supported the children's pragmatic skills (e.g., use of greetings and turn-taking) and literacy skills (e.g., narrative structure of problem and resolution in a sequence).

Vignette 2

Rosanna has been teaching for 10 years and teaching in Years 1 and 2 for the past five years. As part of their inquiry learning topic on sustainability, the children were supported by Rosanna to develop a story board about a real-world problem. Their story began on an island where the native animals, plants and people lived in harmony for thousands and thousands of years. Rosanna provided opportunities for the children to work in small groups to discuss what the play scene would look like then provided them with the resources to build their setting, characters, and plot. The children then built a board using a combination of structured and unstructured objects including trees, fabrics for grass, rocks, and rivers, sticks, blocks, wool and plastic animals (see Figure 9.3).

Rosanna then scaffolded the children by introducing a problem to their story that involved the introduction of "new people" to their island. Throughout the course of the school term, further problems were introduced to their island as a result of the arrival of new people. Again, the children worked in small groups to establish the problems and create solutions. The children built these problems and solutions within their story board using structured and unstructured objects. At times, Rosanna became the play leader by introducing the problem, such as the impact of new people arriving (e.g., building houses, introducing electricity, plastics, wastes, etc.) and the effects on their island (e.g., floods and drought). In one session, Rosanna brought the children to gather around their storyboard which represented beautiful clean rivers, green trees, and housing along the rivers. She then directed the play by adding a problem to their story board by adding a flood to the river using blue paper muffin pans (see Figure 9.4). She modelled the use of object substitution and the introduction of a problem to the story. She then invited the children to solve the newly introduced problem.

Together, the children created a solution by building an underground drainage system into their play scene. This system was built using straws, paper, string, sticks, and brown fabrics that represented the link between above and below ground level. The children then created other problems and developed co-constructed solutions including the establishment of a recycling factory, a native animal reserve, a desalination plant, a flood warning system, and an underground sewerage system.

Figure 9.3 The Island Storyboard play scene at the beginning of the story. Photograph by Louise Paatsch.

Figure 9.4 Teacher-directed addition of a problem. Photograph by Louise Paatsch.

Vignette 2 demonstrates the teacher's pedagogical expertise in supporting children to engage with real-world problems and to resolve these within their play. While the main aim of the project was to meet particular curriculum goals, the children learnt within a play-based approach. Rosanna was often the onlooker and stage manager as she provided the opportunities for child-directed and child-initiated play and set up the environment to encourage critical thinking, creativity, and imagination. She also moved between the roles of play-leader and co-player as she modelled the introduction of a problem to stimulate children's thinking. She used a wide range of teaching strategies such as scaffolding and modelling, and encouraged the children to reflect and co-construct the story. These opportunities not only supported the development of cognitive skills and academic learning goals but also encouraged children to use pragmatic language skills – skills that support social and emotional development. For example, children interacted with peers as they formed small groups. They had to negotiate their roles, take turns, provide alternative views that all children may not have agreed with, take the perspective of others, and be contingent on the contributions made by others. They also reflected on their own learnings and listened to the learnings of others.

Together, these vignettes demonstrate the dynamic nature of this integrated framework in regard to the critical roles teachers play, and the importance of implementing a range of teaching strategies to support children's learning and development through play.

Conclusion

There is a large body of research that has highlighted the critical role of teachers in children's learning. In this chapter we have presented an integrated framework to demonstrate the dynamic and overlapping roles of teachers when supporting children within various play environments – free, guided, co-opted and direct. We also acknowledge that for many primary school teachers who are introducing play in their classrooms for the first time, that such pedagogical expertise may create different roles and disrupt current practices. However, the framework and the vignettes of practice presented in this chapter demonstrate the application of the framework across different classroom contexts and provide a way for teachers to understand these different roles and teaching strategies. We also recommend that teachers work together with their peers and leadership teams to build understandings, skills, and practice to strengthen their pedagogies within a play-based environment – a rich and authentic environment that we argue is important for supporting children's academic, cognitive, linguistic, and social and emotional development.

References

Beecher, B., & Arthur, L. (2001). *Play and literacy in children's worlds*. Primary English Teaching Association.

Brandisauskiene, A., & Bredikyte, M. (2022). Adult actions supporting narrative playworlds in the classroom. *Forum Oświatowe*, 35(2), 31–68. University of Lower Silesia.

Christie, J. F., & Enz, B. (1992). The effects of literacy play interventions on preschoolers' play patterns and literacy development. *Early Education and Development*, 3(3), 205–220.

Creaghe, N. V. (2020). Symbolic play and language acquisition: The dynamics of infant-caretaker communication during symbolic play. Unpublished doctoral dissertation, The Australian National University, Australia.

Danniels, E., & Pyle, A. (2023). Teacher perspectives and approaches toward promoting inclusion in play-based learning for children with developmental disabilities. *Journal of Early Childhood Research*. doi:1476718X221149376.

Gmitrová, V., & Gmitrov, J. (2003). The impact of teacher-directed and child-directed pretend play on cognitive competence in kindergarten children. *Early Childhood Education Journal*, 30, 241–246. doi:10.1023/A:1023339724780.

Hakkarainen, P., Bredikyte, M., Jakkula, K., & Munter, H. (2013). Adult play guidance and children's play development in a narrative play-world. *European Early Childhood Education Research Journal*, 21(2), 213–225. doi:10.1080/1350293X.2013.789189.

Hedegaard, M. (2012). Analysing children's learning and development in everyday settings from a cultural-historical wholeness approach. *Mind, Culture, and Activity*, 19(2), 127–138. doi:10.1080/10749039.2012.665560.

Jay, J. A., & Knaus, M. (2018). Embedding play-based learning into junior primary (Year 1 and 2) curriculum in WA. *Australian Journal of Teacher Education (Online)*, 43(1), 112–126.

Jones, E., & Reynolds, G. (1992). *The play's the thing: Teachers' roles in children's play*. Teachers College Press.

Loizou, E. (2017). Towards play pedagogy: Supporting teacher play practices with a teacher guide about socio-dramatic and imaginative play. *European Early Childhood Education Research Journal*, 25(5), 784–795. doi:10.1080/1350293X.2017.1356574.

Martlew, J., Stephen, C., & Ellis, J. (2011). Play in the primary school classroom? The experience of teachers supporting children's learning through a new pedagogy. *Early Years*, 31(1), 71–83. doi:10.1080/09575146.2010.529425.

Nolan, A., & Paatsch, L. (2018). (Re) affirming identities: Implementing a play-based approach to learning in the early years of schooling. *International Journal of Early Years Education*, 26(1), 42–55. doi:10.1080/09669760.2017.1369397.

Pyle, A., & Danniels, E. (2017). A continuum of play-based learning: The role of the teacher in play-based pedagogy and the fear of hijacking play. *Early Education and Development*, 28(3), 274–289. doi:10.1080/10409289.2016.1220771.

Skene, K., O'Farrelly, C. M., Byrne, E. M., Kirby, N., Stevens, E. C., & Ramchandani, P. G. (2022). Can guidance during play enhance children's learning and development in educational contexts? A systematic review and meta-analysis. *Child Development*, 93(4), 1162–1180. doi:10.1111/cdev.13730.

Sobel, D. M., & Sommerville, J. A. (2010). The importance of discovery in children's causal learning from interventions. *Frontiers in Psychology*, 1, 176. doi:10.3389/fpsyg.2010.00176.

Stagnitti, K., Unsworth, C., & Rodger, S. (2000). Development of an assessment to identify play behaviours that discriminate between the play of typical preschoolers and preschoolers with pre-academic problems. *The Canadian Journal of Occupational Therapy*, 67(5): 291–303. doi:10.1177/000841740006700507.

Utami, A. D., Fleer, M., & Li, L. (2022). The "player" role of the teacher in Playworld creates new conditions for children's learning and development. *International Journal of Early Childhood*, 1–18. doi:10.1007/s13158-022-00333-y.

Veresov, N., Veraksa, N., Gavrilova, M., & Sukhikh, V. (2021). Do children need adult support during sociodramatic play to develop executive functions? Experimental evidence. *Frontiers in Psychology*, 5788. doi:10.3389/fpsyg.2021.779023.

Weisberg, D. S., Hirsh-Pasek, K., & Golinkoff, R. M. (2013). Guided play: Where curricular goals meet a playful pedagogy. *Mind, Brain, and Education*, 7(2), 104–112. doi:10.1111/mbe.12015.

Weisberg, D. S., Hirsh-Pasek, K., Golinkoff, R. M., Kittredge, A. K., & Klahr, D. (2016). Guided play: Principles and practices. *Current Directions in Psychological Science*, 25 (3), 177–182. doi:10.1177/0963721416645512.

Vygotsky, L. S. (1978). *Mind in society: The development of higher mental processes*. Harvard University Press.

Vygotsky, L. S. (1967). Play and its role in the mental development of the child. *Soviet Psychology*, 5(3), 6–18. doi:10.2753/RPO10 61–040505036.

Zosh, J. M., Hirsh-Pasek, K., Hopkins, E. J., Jensen, H., Liu, C., Neale, D., & Whitebread, D. (2018). Accessing the inaccessible: Redefining play as a spectrum. *Frontiers in Psychology*, 9, 1124. doi:10.3389/fpsyg.2018.01124.

10 Assessing and Reporting Play

Assessment is used by teachers to monitor student learning and progress, and to inform teachers about their instructional practices (Pyle et al., 2022). Assessment should be rigorous, authentic and ongoing throughout the year (Department of Education and Training [DET], Victoria, n.d; Pyle et al., 2022). The Australian Curriculum (ACARA, 2020) recommends that teachers assess student learning at different levels and for different purposes. Specifically, assessment should include ongoing formative assessment as well as summative assessment, and includes *assessment of learning* (what the student knows at a particular point in time), *assessment as learning* (involving students in their own learning through scaffolding their metacommunication skills), and *assessment for learning* (combining assessment and teaching). The data gathered from assessments support teachers to understand what students know, and to inform teaching practices that scaffold children to their next level of development – their Zone of Proximal Development (see Chapter 9).

When it comes to play-based education, assessment practices of play ability are a challenge for teachers (Pyle et al., 2022), particularly given that these skills are not specifically highlighted in the Australian Curriculum. For example, Pyle and DeLuca (2017), in a study of 77 early years teachers in Ontario Canada, found a misalignment in teachers' understanding of the purpose of play and what was assessed during periods of play. This challenge is deepened as play assessments are based on assumptions of what play is and how it is conceived, thus resulting in various ways to assess play. Added to these challenges are teachers' understandings of play. In practice, we have found that teachers' understandings range from limited to explicit knowledge of play.

Assessment of play must align with practices in the classroom. Play-based learning aligns "with constructivist theories of learning where children and teachers co-construct knowledge through active participation in meaningful experiences, rather than children being passive recipients of knowledge" (Pyle et al., 2022, pp. 1–2). As discussed in other chapters in this book, play-based learning is conceptualised as a continuum from free play where the child initiates and leads the play; to guided play and inquiry play, where the adults initiate the play and the child leads the play; to collaborative play where play is mutually directed; to playful learning and games where the adult initiates and directs the

DOI: 10.4324/9781003296782-12

learning in a playful atmosphere; and lastly to teacher-directed instruction (Pyle et al., 2022; Zosh et al., 2017; 2018). Of these, guided play has been shown to be more effective for student academic learning outcomes than direct instruction or free play (Pyle et al., 2022; Zosh et al., 2018) (see Chapter 9 for further discussion). So, what is known about assessment during play-based learning in the classroom?

A study in Canada found that a sample of 18 teachers used a variety of assessment approaches such as withdrawing students for direct assessment, embedding assessment in play-based activities, and observational assessment of play (Pyle et al., 2022). Through recordings, interviews, and observations, Pyle et al.'s 2022 study findings showed that teachers fell into three groups: free play (where children engaged in construction and pretend play); teacher-directed play (where the teacher organised activities such as sorting out attributes of snowperson cut-outs), and a combination (where a variety of play opportunities were offered such as free play building structures in a sandpit, guiding children to measure plants in a garden, and a whole group singing game) (Pyle et al., 2022).

Table 10.1 summarises the findings of Pyle et al.'s study. Two teachers in the free play group assessed children continually and informally by observing their play and asking children questions about what they were doing. These teachers assessed children on their individual developmental learning (Pyle et al., 2022). Seven teachers were in the teacher-directed play group where they used formal assessment and templates of learning goals to assess specific academic learning goals. Students were withdrawn during free play periods for standardised or district-created formal assessment, such as phonological awareness, numeracy assessments, teacher-directed checklists, and charts that related to specific curricular goals (Pyle et al., 2022). Nine teachers were in the blended group which implemented a variety of approaches to play-based learning from free to guided, to teacher-directed play activities. Assessment for this group of teachers served many purposes, including academic and developmental learning goals and shaping teachers' practices (Pyle et al., 2022).

Assessment within play-based learning requires teachers to understand the value and purpose of play, use an assessment that is congruent with their understanding, and align assessment practices with their approach. Teachers are trained in assessment of academic skills. Training in assessment of play is not so common. For this reason, this chapter will focus on the assessment of play within a classroom context.

To assess play a teacher requires an understanding of the purpose of play, what play is, and what they are observing and what this means (see Chapters 1–6 for information on the purpose and value of play). The following sections present five play assessments that could be implemented in a classroom. These are: the Pretend Play Checklist for Teachers (Stagnitti & Paatsch, 2018), Mature Play Observation Tool (Germeroth et al., 2019), Play Observed Behaviours Scale (Veraksa et al., 2022), Milestones of Engagement (www.learningseeds.com), and the Penn Interactive Peer Play Scale (McWayne et al., 2002).

Table 10.1 A summary of a study on play-based approaches, assessment, and their critique by Pyle et al., 2022

	Reason for play approach	*Assessments used*	*Comments*
Free Play Child's spontaneous engagement in play such as pretend play	Supporting a child's emotional and social wellbeing, resolving conflicts, problem solving, following rules	Informal: observation of play behaviours, listening to children's dialogue, asking children questions about their play	Child development was the central learning goal. Disconnect between academic learning and play, which is incongruent with contemporary research. Unintrusive and non-systematic documentation of a child's learning.
Teacher-directed Play Highly structured playful learning	Play, directed by a teacher, achieves specific academic learning goals.	Formal assessment: withdrawing children for standardised and teacher-directed assessment, numeracy, phonics, literacy, checklists, learning goals related to curriculum	Many opportunities to collect evidence to monitor student learning. Scope of assessment is limited to structured teacher-based assessment. Limits children's autonomy and decision making, reducing opportunities for sophisticated social and emotional skills such as problem solving and creativity.
Continuum of Play Free, guided, and teacher-directed	A variety of approaches support children's academic and developmental learning.	Informal and formal: conversations with and observations of children during play, photos and videos, checklist of curricula objectives, some standardised assessment	Assessment was integrated into play to support academic and developmental learning. Congruent with play-based learning policies. Teachers require a vast amount of understanding in play-based learning pedagogy and assessment. Requires a balance between activities, teacher involvement vs child-initiated activities.

The Pretend Play Checklist for Teachers (PPCT)

The PPCT assessment by Stagnitti and Paatsch (2018) is based on Vygotsky's constructivist view of play where play provides a zone of proximal development for a child's development (see Chapters 2, 3, and 9). This assessment was developed to support teachers to understand and track children's play, identify children's play strengths, identify what play skills to target, increase a teacher's understanding of play, and to identify children who may need a referral to specialist services for further support. This criterion-referenced assessment is suitable for children aged 4–7 years. It assesses five play skills across nine levels of play. The five play skills assessed are: play stories, sequences of play actions (i.e., how coherent the play is), object substitution (i.e., using an object as something else such as a block for a phone), figurine play (e.g., setting up scenes with figurines), role play (i.e., the child is a character themselves in the play). These play skills reflect pretend or imaginative play ability.

The assessment is designed for use in a classroom where there are play-based activities. Children are observed over 3 × 15-minute sessions, with each session having different play materials. To observe all the skills, the play materials are recommended to be unstructured objects (e.g., blocks, cloth, boxes), role play scenes (e.g., café, home corner), and small toys (e.g., figurines, road mat, doll's house). Play stories and sequences of play actions can be observed across all these different play materials. Object substitution can be observed with unstructured objects, role play can be observed with scenes such as a café, and figurine play can be observed with smaller toys, figurines, road mat, and suchlike. The teacher chooses one to three children to observe over the sessions and also focusses on different play skills each observation session. As teachers become skilled at observation, they will be able to observe many play skills in each session. Training is available through www.learntoplaytherapy.com.

The nine levels of play under each play skill reflect increasing complexity in play. Each level of play is scored with 2, 1, or 0. The teacher observes the children and identifies the child's highest level of skill on the PPCT Assessment Sheet. At the child's highest level of play, the child scores 2 for that level. A score of 2 indicates spontaneous self-initiated play. As the PPCT is a screening test and designed for quick use, all skills below the child's highest level of skill are credited a score of 2. Any skills higher than a child's score of 2 are then observed for either a score of 1 or 0. A score of 1 indicates emerging skill as the child requires support to enact the skill, such as observing peers or following teacher or peer suggestions in order to play. A score of 0 indicates that the skill was not observed. Children who have a total score of 70 to 90 are showing (in order of complexity) developing competence, competent player, or very competent player. Children with scores of 69 or below may require further support.

The PPCT provides teachers with knowledge of what play skills to observe, how those play skills reflect play stories, sequences of play actions, object substitution, figurine play or role play, and the complexity of a child's pretend play ability overall. Research has shown that children with more complex levels of pretend play are more self-regulated (see Chapter 4), have narrative ability (see Chapter 6), and have social capabilities (see Chapter 5). To illustrate the use of the PPCT, we now present a case study of George.

Box 10.1 Assessing George's play using the PPCT

George was 5 years and 6 months old and had just commenced his first year of formal schooling. His parents were isolated and not involved socially with the community. George had not attended preschool. His parents had enrolled him at school because the local GP had encouraged the parents to enrol when George was seen for a chest infection. This doctor had noticed that George was very shy and did not speak. George had now recovered from his infection.

After 2 weeks of settle-in time in the classroom, George's teacher, Ms Smith, noticed that George was shy with unfamiliar adults and with peers. After one more week, she decided to observe his play and complete a PPCT to give her more information about George, which could inform her reporting back to his parents.

Ms Smith observed George over 3 weeks. The first play skill observed was object substitution. Ms Smith observed him during recess where there were objects in the sandpit and also inside the classroom when there was opportunity to observe George engage with blocks. In the sandpit, George wandered over and watched the other children. When one boy started to make a cake, George showed interest and squatted down beside the boy and offered him sand to make a bigger cake, saying "for a big cake". After the cake was cooked (according to the other boy) George found some leaves and decorated the cake. George also found a stick to use as a candle. He then used the stick as a knife and cut pieces of the cake to "eat". As the boys enjoyed "eating" the cake, George used the stick as a person and the "person" "ate" some "cake". Ms Smith observations inside the classroom noted that George could stack blocks, but he didn't join in with others when they were making constructions, he just observed.

The next play skill observed was scripts in play. This is the second observation. With the sandpit observation, Ms Smith had noted that this was a home-based script. Inside the classroom, a shop was set up. George was interested in the shop and came over when other children began to play in the area. He suggested that the shop have specials and he was a customer. Later in the session, he went back to the shop and was the shopkeeper. He played this for 45 minutes and during this time Ms Smith observed that he ran out of merchandise and had to shut the shop while he re-stocked. The next day, George again went to the shop and told his teacher that he was going to be the shopkeeper again but this time his shop was going to be a real estate shop and he was selling houses. He had brought pictures of houses from a newspaper he found at home. Within this observation, Ms Smith noted that George had pre-planned this play and he played in his shop for as long as he could. He had several customers and also became a customer. When he was running the real estate agency, he had two customers (in particular) who presented problems to him. One wanted to see the houses and another customer didn't have enough money to buy the house outright. George extended his play with the customers by suggesting they come back later so he could find solutions for them. For one customer he organised with two children who were constructing a building, if he could bring another child to inspect it. For the other customer Ms Smith observed that George rang the bank and organised a loan for the customer. The customers came back and he: (1) showed one customer the construction, and 2) explained the loan from the bank to the other customer. Both customers were happy. Ms Smith observed that George could maintain play in the shop over 2 weeks and that he created more complex problems to solve.

The third observation included Ms Smith observing George during recess when he was playing superheroes with two other boys. George joined in and added problems to the play with the other boys. For example, he took a figurine from the classroom and explained to the other boys that this character was in trouble, and they had to rescue it.

Over the three observations, Ms Smith noted that George was settling in; however, she had not observed that he sets up scenes and creates stories with toys like garages or fire stations. At these times he just observes what the other children are doing. For example, in the third observation, he watched while three boys created a scene with garages, animals, and blocks. He didn't interact with them but did show interest.

Analysis of George's play using the PPCT

Based on George's case study, the following information was gathered about George's play that would inform Ms Smith about her teaching practices with George.

Play Scripts: George could carry out a consistent story over two weeks and include problems and resolutions to problems. This is based on Ms Smith's observations that George played in the shop area for an extended period and introduced problems and resolutions within his play. This is scored as Level 9 on the PPCT for play scripts, which gives a score of 18 out of a possible 18.

Sequences of Play Action: Ms Smith noted that George could pre-plan and organise his play into complex sequences that included problems and resolutions. This is scored as Level 9 on the PPCT for Sequences of Play Action, which gives a score of 18 out of 18.

Object Substitution: In the first observation Ms Smith observed that George could use the stick for many alternate purposes, but he was not observed creating a new object out of many objects (such as a building or train). This is scored as Level 5 on the PPCT for Object Substitution and gives a score of 10 out of 18.

Doll/Teddy/Figurine Play: Over the three observations, Ms Smith noted that George treated a figurine as alive (because it had to be rescued) and that he could use an abstract character in play (this was the stick as a person in the first observation). George was not observed spontaneously playing with toys to create a scene. He was interested and observed only. This is scored as 1 on Level 6 and 2 from Level 5 and gives a score of 11 out of 18.

Role Play: George played the roles of shopkeeper, customer, and superhero over the observation times. He could maintain a role but would often change roles. This is scored as Level 8 on the PPCT for Role Play and gives a score of 16 out of 18.

George's total score is 73 out of 90, which indicates that George is developing competence in play. Ms Smith has noted George's increasing confidence with peers and in his interactions with adults, and demonstrated important pragmatic language skills such as initiation, turn-taking, and topic maintenance (see Chapter 3). The PPCT has identified that George requires more support in extending his play abilities in object substitution and creation of story scenes with toys. Ms Smith is able to use these assessment results to inform her planning and teaching practices with George. Object substitution encourages divergent thinking and creativity (see Chapter 6) and the creation of story scenes involves storytelling with characters, which will encourage narrative, social-emotional capabilities, and theory of mind (see Chapters 4 and 5). Ms Smith will re-assess George in six months to monitor his progress.

Mature Play Observation Tool (MPOT)

The Mature Play Observation Tool (Germeroth et al., 2019) focusses on make-believe or pretend play ability of children within a classroom setting. It is designed for children in preschool and the early years of primary school, although the Germeroth et al. (2019) study focussed on research for 4–5-year-old children. They argued that to assess play development teachers must be able to observe how and when children engage in play and identify distinct play behaviours in social settings with peers (Germeroth et al., 2019). This observation tool includes child play behaviours and teachers' interaction with children within a classroom setting.

The MPOT includes descriptions of mature make-believe play and immature make-believe play across four levels for five Child Dimensions and three Adult Dimensions. The Child Dimensions include: Child-Created Props (the extent to which children create props and gestures to support their play); Child Meta-Play (includes metacommunication such as children's talk on how and what they will be playing as well as communication about roles, rules and the use of props in the play); Play Interaction (social interactions between children); Children's Role Playing (role play); Child Role Speech and Communication During Play (includes oral language and gestures to communicate the meaning in the play). The Adult

Dimensions are: Centre Management (how a teacher uses systems – e.g., concept maps, pictures – to support self-regulated play); Make-Believe Play Time (time allocated to uninterrupted play); and Teacher Intervention (the extent to which adults intervene during play). Each item is scored on a 4-level scale of maturity, for example, object-centred role play (where object-oriented actions determine roles) is Level 1; Level 4 is elaborate relationship-centred play (where roles are well defined, and children are aware of the rules of the play). Details of categories and scoring of this assessment are quoted from an unpublished manual (Bodrova et al., 2012).

The MPOT is designed to evaluate play quality at the classroom level (Germeroth et al., 2019, p. 213) and is not designed for making direct inferences about individual children's play maturity. This assessment considers teacher or adult interactions and children's level of make-believe play maturity.

Play Observed Behaviours Scale (POBS)

This scale was devised for teachers in Russia for widespread, quick use. The authors (Veraksa et al., 2022) noted that Russian teachers have large administrative loads, large classes, a rigid, fixed daily routine, and that opportunities for special training on play assessment were limited. However, teachers could assess each child's propensity to lead the play, to what extent they followed rules, and whether children had preferences for play topics (Veraksa et al., 2022, p. 4). These three aspects of play could be matched to Vygotsky's theories relating to executive function. That is, greater cognitive flexibility may be associated with a child's ability to initiate play with others; a child with a narrow range of play preferences may indicate lower cognitive flexibility; and if a child conforms to rules it may be indicative of working memory and inhibition (Veraksa et al., 2022).

The Play Observed Behaviours Scale is a short teacher survey, which was designed to be used by Russian teachers who taught children aged 6–7 years. The survey has eight items which are scored across a 3-point Likert type scale. A score of 1 indicates the play behaviour was never expressed by the child. A score of 2 indicates the play behaviour was observed occasionally by the teacher, and a score of 3 indicates the child was observed frequently expressing the play behaviour (Veraksa et al., 2022).

The eight items are (Veraksa et al., 2022, p. 4):

1   The child leads the play.
2   Peers gladly include the child in their play.
3   The child has conflicts with peers during play.
4   The child understands and follows the rules of play.
5   The child makes sure peers comply with the rules of play.
6   The child likes to engage in games with explicit rules in free time.
7   The child likes to engage in quiet projects or activities in free time.
8   The child likes to play/act out stories in free time.

The POBS had good internal reliability (Chronbach's alpha = .76). They found that Russian children's play leadership (initiation) increased with age, and play preferences and rule conformity decreased by age 7 years (Veraksa et al., 2022). Children who performed highly on leadership, preferences, and conformity also scored well in executive function tasks, except visual working memory (Veraksa et al., 2022).

Milestones of Engagement

The Milestones of Engagement was developed by Erica Key and Learning Seeds in Boston, USA. It is designed to identify engagement and opportunities for support during observations of play in group activities and classrooms for individual children aged 2 to 6 years. Hence it is suitable for those who have entered formal schooling in Australia. Children are observed minute to minute (referred to as "time-stamping" by Learning Seeds) over 90 minutes during times of transition between activities, and in open-ended play indoors and outdoors. (These times are often referred to as Centre Time, Choice Time, Free Play Time, and Recess.) During the observations of the children, the target child's activities are compared to the group. For example, if a group is debating what to build in the block area and the target child is looking away and not contributing, this would be noted for follow up and action. Table 10.2 presents the eight types of play that are observed using this framework.

The information gathered using the Milestones of Engagement are examples of the child's engagement and disengagement across the eight areas (see Table 10.2). From the observations, goals can be set for the child to provide new and extended experiences in the classroom. Goals may also be developed for children who are disconnected from the group. For the struggling child, the adult observes which of the engagement areas are dominant. For example, a child with sensory avoidance may have limited engagement in the environment, which prevents them from engaging in most of the upper-level experiences, such as social interaction or pretend play. Another example would be a child who is not yet showing social motivation and may be very object-focused with lots of activity that is repetitive. Goals for this child would be to make connections for the child between preferred objects and social experiences in the social realms of transaction, interaction, and pretend play.

The Milestones of Engagement allows observers of a child to identify the various types of engagement available to a child in a group experience during exploration or open-ended play when children are free to use materials, make choices, have conversations, and engage in pretending. The Learning Seeds team considers both the child's observed motivation and engagement, and the practitioner's goals to engage the child in deeper or more interactive experiences so the child can expand their motivation, habits, and skills for connecting, learning, and playing with the group. In addition to the Milestones of Engagement provided below, Learning Seeds notes the various observable motivators exhibited by a child. These are: **Solitary** Disengaged – Avoidance and Withdrawal (the child seeks to disconnect through leaving, ignoring or isolating in non-productive

Table 10.2 Milestones of Engagement by Learning Seeds. Reprinted with permission of Erica Key and Learning Seeds Inc., a Social Benefit Corporation

Experience	Learning Seeds definition	Current experience (some guiding questions provided)	What can we help the child experience next?
Environment	Formal places like rooms and play boundaries, semi-formal places like group tables and seating around a rug, and informal places like bodies in the group and hub of the play, proximity to peers	Is the child entering the environment, staying at the door or edges of the space, or bolting from the environment? Does the child sit in proximity to peers with their body facing materials? What is the child missing in the environment?	
Solitary and Parallel Activities	Object and sensory exploration, crafts, movement, games, routines, representational play, structured tasks, classroom rituals, object and sensory exploration, following directions	Does the child choose an activity available and settle into engagement with the activity, or do they move quickly from one activity to another? Does the child explore new novel materials? Does the child try new actions or welcome new uses of objects? Is the child doing activities with parallels to others (facing others, in the same space, using the same materials, etc.)? What is the child missing in activities?	
Solitary Pretend Play	Adding stories to objects, using objects to represent other things, making two "character" objects speak to each other	Does the child use objects to represent other things? Does the child add story or actions to the play?	
Transactions	Getting needs met, navigating explicit group rules, cultural norms, experiencing agency, naming and revealing systems, discovering what you can choose and what you cannot, participating in structured group transitions; making hidden rules visible for navigating classroom routines, supplies, and expectations. Making multi-step plans that help a child see how their needs will be met if they first meet some expectation of the group/teacher/etc.	Does the child correctly seek out help? Does the child have an effective way to say no, or do they refuse with ignoring or big upsets? Does the child follow group norms (allow everyone to take Legos from a communal bin, use class systems to get a turn with an activity, wait for turns and understands how turns/class schedule works)?	

Experience	Learning Seeds definition	Current experience (some guiding questions provided)	What can we help the child experience next?
Reactions and Shared Experiences	Lock-eyed laughter, understanding other people's facial expressions and how they come about, laughing together, causing others to feel feelings, being near others and having basic proximity for the sake of companionship	Does the child look to see peers' reactions to their actions? Does the child look to see if peers are looking at the same thing as them? Does the child seek and use facial expressions to connect?	
Interactions	Discussions, chats, topical conversations, content discussions	Does the child respond to questions? Does the child chime in when others make comments? Does the child initiate conversation with peers? Does the child listen to peer's responses and use key words from the other person in their reply? Can the child negotiate?	
Interactive Pretend Play	Back and forth, co-created, pretend play with roles, activities, and imagined settings; giving and following directions that enhance the shared play; developing logical sequences of actions to help the play develop into a story	Does the child seem to tolerate and enjoy play with pretend use of objects, roles, settings, and actions? Does the child create roles for themself in play? Does the child recognise and tolerate the pretend roles of others? Does the child incorporate peers' ideas into the play? Does the child plan out sequences of play with peers?	
Belonging, Identity, and Self-awareness	Development of identity – group and individual/metacognition/temporal processing/perspective taking and thinking about the moment from a bird's eye view, confidence (being aware of what you know how to do)	Does the child understand that "the group has thoughts about me?" Can the child think about the past and present to plan for the future? Can the child take the perspective of others? Does the child reflect on behaviours and change them to change the outcome?	

ways); **Solitary** Engaged – Object Seeking (the child engages with materials or activities in the room but with most attention to objects vs people); **Transactional** (seeking agency, getting the child's own basic needs met, learning to navigate the choices, consequences, and basic information in the routines of the group); and **Interactive** (the child seeks a variety of social reactions and facial expressions, seeks chats/joking/conversations, appreciates negotiation, and finally shares increasingly complex role-based pretend play). Further observations and notes are made regarding the child's interests and uses of objects; the child's reactions, interactions, and conversations; and if pretend play is absent, solitary, or social.

From this baseline of information, the adults can provide scaffolded experiences for the child that connect with the child's current motivation while providing exposure to deeper or more social engagement experiences. By deepening and extending the child's experiences, children get to practice social interaction skills in ways that create more authentic opportunities to connect with the group. Once a child is able to engage in the more complex experiences of holding back and forth **interactions** and engaging in **interactive pretend play**, the child can then learn through metacognition how to further improve their group experience. This framework is especially beneficial for students who do not yet have mastery of the complex skills required for reflecting on one's own past behaviour to plan for improvements in the future. This framework can help educators identify instances where a child is naturally engaged and what experiences can help support a more inclusive and pro-social experience. These scaffolded experiences also support children to develop mature social and emotional learning skills, including: metacognition, temporal processing, perspective taking, and executive functioning. The following link demonstrates the Milestones of Engagement with a video presentation of a child case study. https://www.learning seeds.com/enlightened-shadowing

The following vignette using the Milestones of Engagement describes a child's engagement progressing from Solitary and Parallel Activities, to Shared Experiences to Interactive Pretend Play using "tips" from Learning Seeds. During playground time, Student J is swinging on his belly, with his arms out wide like an airplane. A peer is doing the same thing next to him, but the two are not interacting. Student J seems happy to simply remain in proximity to a peer (Solitary and Parallel Activities). The adult begins using a tip called "Group Language Creates Group Connections", by saying "The pilots are flying! Pilots, where are you two pilots going?" This causes some eye contact and glances and shared smiles between the two peers (Reactions and Shared Experiences). The swings slow down. The adult's scaffolding of the student's brief interaction provides an opportunity to extend the students' experience. To ensure the Shared Experience evolves into more connection instead of fading to a stop, as the swings slow down the adult uses a tip called "Unison Triggers" and tells the two peers that they have to take off in their planes at the exact same time. She prompts them to count "3, 2, 1, take off!" The two count down together and increase their eye contact in order to count in sync, and then begin swinging again together, looking at one another and laughing. To build from these Shared Experiences to Interaction and Pretending, the adult introduces a problem into the play that will encourage deeper collaboration between the peers. The adult uses a tip called "Be a Side Guide in the Play" and pretends to be in the role of air traffic controller, pretending to radio to each of the planes. She inserts a problem into the play and adds fun to it by using a tip called "Oh No You Don't", saying "Oh dear, I hope you pilots don't hit turbulence!" Both peers pretend to hit turbulence, and report that their planes need repairs. At this point, Student J is now using eye contact, exchanging expressions, listening to peer's comments and is immersed in a shared pretend problem they are solving together. Thanks to the support of the adult, the child is now experiencing Interactive Pretend Play. The two children continue the play, repairing their planes, and flying back to air traffic control together.

Penn Interactive Peer Play Scale (PIPPS)

The Penn Interactive Peer Play Scale (McWayne et al., 2002) teacher rating scale is a behavioural rating scale to assist in understanding peer play behaviours of children in the classroom and at school. It was designed for peer play assessment of children in high-risk urban areas in the USA (McWayne et al., 2002). The PIPPS has several purposes, including: to assess children's play during free play sessions; to create a common language between teachers and parents; to inform curriculum; and to evaluate classroom interventions.

The PIPPS has 32 items, and each item is scored using one of four responses: 1 = never, 2 = seldom, 3 = often, and 4 = always. The assessment takes approximately 10–15 minutes to complete for each child (McWayne et al., 2002). The 32 items can be categorised into three dimensions: (1) Play Interaction (indicates a child's play strengths such as helping others, creativity, inclusiveness); (2) Play Disruption (aggressive, antisocial behaviours); and (3) Play Disconnection (withdrawn and non-participatory play). Examples of items for Play Interaction are "helps other children", and "positive emotion during play". Examples of Play Disruption items are "starts fights and arguments", and "grabs other things". Examples of Play Disconnection items are "withdraws", and "wanders aimlessly". The child's scores can be compared to standard scores.

In studies where teachers have filled out the PIPPS independently from researchers, who assessed children using the Child-Initiated Pretend Play Assessment (Stagnitti, 2022), it was found that children who struggled to substitute objects in play were more likely to be socially disruptive with peers (McAloney & Stagnitti, 2009; Uren & Stagnitti, 2009). If a child struggled to elaborately sequence their play actions, they were more likely to be disconnected from peers, and if a child could initiate elaborate sequences of play actions and substitute objects in play, they were more likely to be scored as socially interactive by teachers (McAloney & Stagnitti, 2009; Uren & Stagnitti, 2009).

Documenting learning and reporting on play

Once teachers have decided on the play assessment they will use in their classroom, it will be important to consider the ways in which the children's learning will be documented, and to whom the findings will be reported, including parents, other teachers, and the children themselves. The following sections of this chapter will present some considerations and practical examples for documenting learning and reporting.

Documenting learning

Teachers implement various ways of collecting evidence to record children's learning. In the case of documenting children's play abilities, it is important to capture this learning in authentic contexts as it occurs naturally.

Documenting learning can take many forms. Teachers may observe the children's play skills and complete the assessments in-situ. For example, they may complete the checklists or assessment forms as they observe the children in their play. At times, this practice may present some challenges for teachers, especially when they must attend to the needs of all children in their class. However, having other supportive adults in the classroom at the time of undertaking this assessment can assist teachers to complete these assessments successfully.

Over the years, we have found that one of the most powerful and effective ways to collect samples of children's play abilities is to video record the session. Such data can be used to observe more than one child in a given play session. Teachers can use the video and audio recording to complete the play assessment at another time. In addition, these videos can be used to assess children's learning across other curriculum learning areas such as English, Mathematics, Science, and the Arts (see Chapter 7 for further discussion regarding ways for observing other learning areas in children's play).

Video recordings may also be used to stimulate discussions with other teachers. For example, teachers could use the videos to moderate the assessment of children's play by discussing their observations and scoring of particular skills, through rich collegial conversations that support their understandings of play and play skills, and to build teacher knowledge and confidence. The following example presents a discussion between two Foundation teachers after they had taken video samples of the children's play.

David and Monique have been teaching together in the Foundation year for the past three years. The classrooms are in an open-plan space and both teachers team-teach for most parts of the day except during specialist times such as Health and Physical Education and Languages. The school has implemented a play-based approach in the Foundation to Year 2 classes. Over the past week, David and Monique video recorded the children over three play sessions prior to completing the PPCT (Stagnitti & Paatsch, 2018). During their planning time, both teachers scored the PPCT independently using the video of the children playing in the pretend supermarket. They then came together to moderate to ensure accuracy in their scoring. The scoring for the play skill of object substitution showed differing results. David had scored Emmanuel higher (Level 8 – uses any object for anything) than Monique (Level 5 – uses the same object for lots of things). Following this revelation of the discrepancy between scores, a rich discussion ensued where they used the video to show why they had scored the child the way they did.

DAVID: Let's watch the video at the spot where Emmanuel is playing the role of the person at the checkout. [David narrates what he sees on the video, saying the following] He put all the groceries through the scanner using all the objects that the other child, Ella, had placed in the basket. Some were toy food objects, some were blocks and sticks. Emmanuel realised that he didn't have a till to put the money in so went and collected a box and returned to the play scene. He then used the same box to put the groceries in for Ella to take home. He then uses the same box as a fridge and put some other groceries inside. That's right, isn't it?

MONIQUE: Yes, but that is an example of Level 5 – uses the same object for lots of things. I wouldn't say that he uses any object for anything. Isn't it the same object?

DAVID: Yes, but let's keep watching as I think he is using any object for anything. Remember he used that other block, you know, that pyramid-shaped one to …

MONIQUE: [Overlapping and interrupting David] Yeah yeah, that's right. Emmanuel picked that up and used it for a QR code scanner then picked up the red piece of fabric and pretended it was meat as he restocked the fridge. But don't you think that he copied Olivia? See here [goes back to an earlier part of the video where Olivia is doing the same thing]. I think that we should then score Emmanuel at Level 8 but only as emerging as I am not sure that he has established spontaneously. Maybe we need to observe further?

This example shows the ways in which the two teachers negotiated and moderated as they watched the video together while scoring the child's object substitution play skills. The video provided evidence for their discussion and supported each other's understandings of the play skills. They acknowledged the need to collect further evidence and worked collaboratively to come to a consensus.

Monique and David also uploaded this video into their ePortfolios to maintain a permanent record of the children's learning over time. They also used these videos to talk with the children about their learning, as well as with the children's parents during parent–teacher interviews.

Reporting children's play abilities

Reporting on children's learnings of particular play skills in a form that is beneficial to parents, teachers, and children is important for celebrating what has been achieved, supporting a shared understanding of the learning goal, and for planning of strategies and experiences to scaffold the child to the next level. Schools will have their own ways of reporting for other curriculum learning areas, and we argue that reporting on children's play abilities is also critical.

Over the years we have observed many reporting practices in various schools. Below, we present three examples of the ways schools have reported play abilities to children, teachers, and parents.

School 1: Use of the PPCT scoring sheet

Teachers used the one PPCT scoring sheet for each child for the year. Throughout the year they would add a new skill that they may have observed, using a different colour marker and recording the date that the play skill was achieved. This score sheet was added to the child's report and then discussed with the parents at parent–teacher interviews. Prior to being sent home to parents, teachers had provided a professional learning session for parents at a parent night. They also recorded the session and uploaded it into the parent portal on the school's website.

School 2: "I can"

Teachers developed an "I Can" child report using the play skills outlined in the PPCT. They turned each descriptor for all five play skills at all nine levels into an "I Can" statement. For example, in the play skill Role Play, the following are examples of the "I Can" statements created:

(I) I can watch others.
(II) I can copy an adult or a friend.
(III) I can do other actions that I have seen my teacher or my friend do.

The teachers recorded the date that these were achieved by each child. Only the "I Can" statements that the child had achieved were included in the child's report to parents. All reports were uploaded into the child's ePortfolio in digital form.

School 3:Data walls

Many schools use "data walls" to show children's progress over time. Typically, this involves listing the Content Descriptors or Achievement Standard (some schools have also included elaborations, although our observation of this practice was usually in schools with small numbers of students) for each level for each learning area on a wall. A photo of each child is then placed on the achievement and level. As the child achieves each level their photo is moved to the corresponding standard.

Some schools have located these data walls in staff rooms or staff areas, while other schools have located them in the classroom where the children place their own photo on their achievement for each area as it is reached. Often the data walls are presented as "I Can" statements or as learning goals.

In School 3, play skills were included as an additional learning area on the data wall in the staffroom and in the classroom. Again, this school used versions of the descriptors outlined in the PPCT and placed a photo of each child in the class on the area that they were currently working on as their learning goal (i.e., those scored as either 1 – emerging, or 0 – not evident). These recordings of children's play abilities were also presented to the parents in the child's school report using the same ratings as those used to report other curriculum learning areas (e.g., "satisfactory", "above satisfactory", "below satisfactory"; or "at standard", "above standard", "below standard").

In all three examples, all schools valued the importance of including play as a learning area that needed to be assessed, recorded, and reported. All had varying practices, but together the examples present different ways that one play assessment, the PPCT (Stagnitti & Paatsch, 2018), could be modified for the purpose of reporting to parents, teachers, and children. Such practices could be adapted to other play assessments that schools decide to use as part of the assessment protocols across the year levels.

Conclusion

There are many assessments of play but only a few play assessments which have been developed for use by teachers in a classroom. This chapter has given five examples of play assessments that were developed for school use.

Germeroth et al. (2019) noted that "direct observation [of children's make-believe or pretend play] provides more valid data than other methods such as interviews or questionnaires" (p. 187). Play assessments for teachers that utilise direct observation provide teachers with opportunities to observe children's play more closely, consequently strengthening their skills in the identification of when play occurs and the quality of children's play. The latter being pertinent when play assessments have levels of complexity of play to observe.

Direct observation of children's play may also provide opportunities for teachers to observe children's quality of play along with other abilities such as self-regulation and social interaction, as well as other curricular learning areas. In this chapter we have also highlighted the importance of gathering data to record children's learning, and the different ways to report these findings to children, teachers, and parents. The information gleaned from observations of children's play, combined with outcomes from conversations with teachers, children, and parents, can be used to inform future learning goals and teacher practices to support children's play and learning.

References

Australian Curriculum, Assessment and Reporting Authority (ACARA). (2020). retrieved February 2023. https://www.australiancurriculum.edu.au/f-10-curriculum/.

Bodrova, E., Björk, C., Day-Hess, C., Germeroth, C., Maxxio, D., & Isaacs, S. (2012). *Scaffolding early learning: Strategies for success.* Unpublished manual, Mid-continent Research for Education and Learning (McREL), Denver CO.

Department of Education and Training [DET] Victoria. Retrieved February2023. https://www.education.vic.gov.au/school/teachers/teachingresources/practice/Pages/learning-assessment-and-reporting.aspx.

Germeroth, C., Bodrova, E., Day-Hess, C., Barker, J., Sarama, J., Clements, D., & Layzer, C. (2019). Play it high, play it low: Examining the reliability and validity of a new observation tool to measure children's make-believe play. *American Journal of Play*, 11, 183–221. https://files.eric.ed.gov/fulltext/EJ1211531.pdf.

McAloney, K., & Stagnitti, K. (2009). Pretend play and social play: The concurrent validity of the Child-Initiated Pretend Play Assessment. *International Journal of Play Therapy*, 18(2), 99–113. doi:10.1037/a0014559.

McWayne, C., Sekino, Y., Hampton, G., & Fantuzzo, J. (2002). *Penn Interactive Peer Play Scale (PIPPS)*. University of Pennsylvania.

Pyle, A. & DeLuca, C. (2017). Assessment in play-based kindergarten classrooms: An empirical student of teacher perspectives and practices. *Journal of Educational Research*, 110, 457–466. doi:10.1080/00220671.2015.111800.

Pyle, A., DeLuca, C., Wickstrom, H., & Danniels, E. (2022). Connecting kindergarten teachers' play-based learning profiles and their classroom assessment practices. *Teaching and Teacher Education*, 119. doi:10.1016/j.tate.2022.103855.

Stagnitti, K. (2022). *Child-Initiated Pretend Play Assessment 2* (2nd edn). Learn to Play.

Stagnitti, K. & Paatsch, L. (2018). *Pretend Play Checklist for Teachers*. Learn to Play. https://www.learntoplayevents.com/product/pretend-play-checklist-for-teachers-ppc-t-manual/.

Uren, N., & Stagnitti, K. (2009). Pretend play, social competence and involvement in children aged 5–7 years: The concurrent validity of the Child-Initiated Pretend Play Assessment. *Australian Occupational Therapy Journal*, 56(1), 33–40. doi:10.1111/j.1440-1630.2008.00761.x.

Veraksa, A., Bukhalenkova, D., Almazova, O., Sukhikh, V., & Colliver, Y. (2022). The relationship between Russian kindergarteners' play and executive functions: Validating the Play Observed Behavioural Scale. *Frontiers in Psychology*, 13, 1–12. doi:10.3389/fpsyg.2022.797531.

Zosh, J., Hirsh-Pasek, K., Hopkins, E., Jensen, H., Liu, C., Neale, D., Solis, L. & Whitebread, D. (2018). Assessing the inaccessible: Redefining play as a spectrum. *Frontiers in Psychology*, 9, 1–12. doi:10.3389/fpsyg.2018.01124.

Zosh, J., Hopkins, E., Jensen, H., Liu, C., Neale, D., Hirsh-Pasek, K., Solis, L., & Whitebread, D. (2017). *Learning through play: A review of the evidence*. The LEGO Foundation. ISBN: 978-987-999589-999581-7

11 Practical Suggestions and Examples of Children Learning Through Play

Throughout this book, we have provided excerpts to illustrate specific aspects of learning through play, as well as practical in-class examples of play-based learning. In this chapter, we provide more examples of using play to calm and settle children in order to learn, as well as two vignettes. The two vignettes are from St James Parish School in Victoria, Australia. This school has refined learning through play over 17 years, with positive academic results. We begin this chapter by sharing practical activities used by teachers in classrooms to help calm children, so they are ready to learn. In this first section, these activities are presented in neurodevelopmental order: 1. Meeting basic needs and creating a sense of safety, 2. Engaging the senses, 3. Feeling ready, 4. Abstract thought and complex problem-solving. Some frequently asked questions bring the chapter to a close.

Play activities to prepare children to learn

Recapping from Chapter 2, children need to feel safe in order to learn. The social engagement system is activated when we use a gentle steady voice, smile with our eyes, are calm ourselves, and have an open body posture. This sense of safety is strengthened when school staff engage with children as capable beings who can learn and grow. Playful teacher interactions have been shown to increase children's learning (Zosh et al., 2018). By playing and laughing together, engaging children joyfully in learning, and showing empathy, the release of the neuropeptide oxytocin is encouraged, enhancing feelings of well-being and trust (Stewart et al., 2016). Some practical activities that teachers can use that target particular needs and behaviours of students are now discussed.

Firm foundations: play that meets basic needs and creates a sense of safety

A classroom that feels safe supports all other learning. As noted in Chapter 2, a classroom that feels safe contributes to reduced stress for students and teachers, improving learning outcomes for the whole class. Sometimes students experience early negative life experiences that can lead to changes in brain development (Siegel & Bryson, 2012). These can result in increased problems with physical

DOI: 10.4324/9781003296782-13

health, relationships, learning, and self-regulation (Brandt et al., 2014; Perry, 2013). Teachers may notice students who are tired, have poor appetites, or difficulty focussing.

For these students, allow flexibility in your classroom around food and water breaks. Students can benefit from self-awareness activities and visualisation, such as closing their eyes and noticing how each part of their body feels from their feet to their heads (not forgetting internal organs such as their stomach and heart). Age-appropriate yoga is also becoming popular in many classrooms. Sue Jennings (2017) has a selection of activities with reproducible worksheets in her book *Creative Play for Children at Risk*, that would benefit students in early years classrooms to improve self-awareness.

Including clear and predictable routines and student directed activities helps the brain reorganise and relearn the skills that support integration of the Reptilian and Emotional Brain (lower, subconscious brain function, see Chapter 2) with higher levels of conscious brain function (Perry et al., 2000; Siegel & Bryson, 2012; Siegel, 2012). Playful activities that assist teachers with creating a sense of calm and safety include the use of soft music (played in the background), singing familiar rhymes/songs, gentle massage or touch (e.g., gentle handshakes, or, sitting in a circle children draw slowly on the back of a child in front of them with their fingertips) (Perry et al., 2000). Further activities that teachers use to support children to settle, to learn and feel a sense of safety include: drumming and rhythm/clapping games to help regulate heartbeat, offering of a high-five with eye contact to improve relationships and connection, taking turns with slow and gentle blowing of a cotton ball to regulate breathing, tasting and smelling games, playing in sand or with clay (Perry et al., 2000).

The classroom environment can be adapted to provide safe spaces, like cubby houses or cushioned nooks. These spaces can be individualised and be available for children who need to retreat at times when they are overwhelmed (encouraging self-regulation). This assists students who have difficulties with transitions, struggle to regulate emotions, have sensory sensitivities, anxiety or trauma symptoms, a known diagnosis, or other environmental challenges. For children with sensitivities to noise, earmuffs or headphones (with or without music) may help to settle the child. Weighted blankets or a toy to cuddle may help calm some children who are unsettled (also see the TECA trauma checklist in Chapter 2).

Engaging students by engaging the senses

When students in the classroom are feeling safe, familiar with routines, and are able to focus, but are struggling to connect or control their movements, activities that stimulate the senses target the lower areas of the brain (Perry et al., 2000). Play activities, such as, the use of clay, sand, playdough, scent-guessing games, and art activities are relevant here. Singing and moving to music, reading with rhythm (e.g., *Mem Fox* and *Dr Seuss* books) and guided imagery can be included in learning experiences. Story Dogs is an Australian charity that supports early literacy and reading skill development, see: https://www.storydogs.org.au/ for details.

An animal in the classroom can be beneficial to provide an opportunity for connection with learning materials, in a safe and non-judgemental way (Brelsford et al., 2017).

Feeling ready: playing to build social skills, emotional regulation, self-esteem, and resilience

This section considers play-based activities that provide opportunities for emotional self-regulation in your classroom. Play-based learning that enhances social capabilities can include groups of students engaging in role play, figurine play, play scenes that encourage sharing and dividing food (e.g., a corner of the room set up with a pretend café), or serving others (e.g., a shop with a cash register and play money) (see also Chapters 5 and 6). A classroom activity that investigates facial expressions using mirrors, or drawing emotions, provides children with information on naming emotions, which integrates brain function (Siegel & Bryson, 2012).

Thought and complex problem solving: playing for cognitive flexibility and strength

The Rational Brain (cortex and neocortex, also see Chapter 2) is the last to integrate in humans and this part of the brain helps us to rationalise, reason, moderate our behaviour, and solve complex problems. Students benefit from increased opportunities to engage in learning through the Rational Brain, integrating lower functions in the brain with higher functions. Activities like storytelling and stories with metaphors, dance and drama, role play, discussions about excursions/ experiences, expressive music, arts, riddles and problem-solving games, strategy and team building games, humour, and insight-oriented activities can help to enhance development in this area (Perry et al., 2000). See also Chapters 5 and 6 for examples of storytelling through play-based learning.

Throughout this book, the continuum of play has been referred to, where learning is more effective when students experience a sense of agency and contribute to learning experiences. This approach impacts on the role of the teacher, which is explored in detail in Chapter 9. An example of collectively created learning experiences is a project on the history of language (see Box 11.2). The children at St James Parish School were using play scenes to act out an historical story that the teacher was guiding. As the story progressed, the students became shocked by the vicious treatment of the Saxons by the Vikings. The students advised the teacher that they felt that the Vikings could have handled the situation more amicably – so the teacher supported the students to lead, and to rewrite parts of the story. The students acted out a negotiation between the Vikings and the Saxons, that did not involve war or killing, and saved the Saxons from devastating consequences. This provided a rich learning experience on the importance and power of negotiation, expression of empathy, and a very high level of play development for the young students. The next section provides further examples on play-based learning from St James Parish School.

Practical examples of play-based learning over a year

The following vignettes have been provided by St James Parish School in Victoria, Australia, which has over 17 years of experience in embedding play in learning. Staff have created many play-based learning experiences, for example, the island story includes children in the early years, guided by their teacher in a story of an island and the problems encountered when new people came to live on the island. Within this play scenario, there were maths, science, and engineering problems to tackle so the island could be environmentally sustainable, and the people could live in harmony.

The vignettes explain in more depth how play is embedded in the learning for children, with examples of projects that span a whole year. These are presented in Box 11.1 and Box 11.2.

Box 11.1 The ecology of fairy tales
By Peter Fahey, Courtney Mogensen, and Jacqui Jarvis

Teachers designed, and co-produced with the children, a project titled The Ecology of Fairy Tales, using a storyboard, which represented eight traditional fairy tales. Storyboards provide a "big picture" context within which the children link information from various curriculum areas.

The storyboard took the form of a two-storey tree, where the roots of the tree represented traditional fairy tales that have endured through time. The growth above ground played host to fractured fairy tale versions (see Figures 11.1 to 11.4). The leafy canopy of the tree evolved, holding the stories the children created. Just as trees rely on the mycorrhizal network, children's abilities to produce their personal narratives relied on a deep knowledge of the narrative structure. The storyboard provided meaningful correlation with spelling, vocabulary, fluency, and comprehension.

Symbolic play pieces were used on the storyboard when traditional fairy tales were introduced. When being exposed to the fractured fairy tales, conventional play pieces were used (see Figures 11.2 to 11.4).

The children spent two to three weeks familiarising and engaging themselves with traditional fairy tales; grammatical patterns, tenses, characters, settings, problem sequences, and vocabulary. Over time the children's stories began to change. They contained more fictional characters, emotive language was used to describe the characters' actions, several problems began to appear with logical sequences and resolutions. Children were presented with fractured fairy tales to compare and contrast using the story grammar bookmark as a reference.

Throughout the course of the project the children had access to prompts and domain knowledge from teachers. They were not left on their own to explore and discover ideas but were guided through well-designed activities and questions that prompted them to build the necessary knowledge.

Figure 11.1 The two-story tree used in the Ecology of Fairy Tales. Photograph by Jacqui Jarvis. Used with permission.

Second, the children still received instruction after they built up necessary background knowledge. Guided learning enabled understanding of the deep structure of concepts, better knowledge retention, and transfer to other contexts.

Figure 11.2 Detail of the base of the two-storey tree showing a jungle scene. Photograph by Jacqui Jarvis. Used with permission.

Figure 11.3 Detail of the base of the two-storey tree showing a beach scene. Photograph by Jacqui Jarvis. Used with permission.

Figure 11.4 Detail at the base of the two-storey tree showing a town scene. Photograph by Jacqui Jarvis. Used with permission.

The children collaborated in teams across several dilemmas introduced on the storyboard. Each child was represented on the board by a character (avatar) from either a traditional or twisted fairy tale.

Children were exposed to the following fairy tales:

- *The Three Little Pigs* by Kath Jewitt
- *The Truth about the Three Little Pigs* by Jon Scieszka
- *Little Red Riding Hood* by Gaby Goldsack
- *Ninja Red Riding Hood* by Corey Rosen Schwartz
- *Goldilocks and The Three Bears* by Sarah Delmege
- *Goldilocks and The Three Dinosaurs* by Mo Willems
- *Three Billy Goats Gruff* by George Bridge
- *Just Another Friendly Troll* by Alvin Granowsky
- *The Gingerbread Man* by Dona Herweck Rice
- *Catch that Cookie – Scavenger Hunt* by Hallie Durand

Rubrics were used by teachers to describe the learning intentions for the students. Learning intentions is a general term describing either objectives, goals, or aims. The rubrics were valuable as they communicated with the children that learning takes place over time and not in a single encounter or lesson. Rubrics were situated next to Models of Excellence in the classroom. The combination enabled the children to better understand the learning intention.

Once children could easily retell many of the eight fairy tales, features began to change. Whilst some children wrestled with the complexity of changing one feature, such as changing the problem or the ending, other children demonstrated the ability to superimpose a different character or setting such as Goldilocks getting lost in the story of The Three Little Pigs.

Figure 11.5 The café play space. Photograph by Jacqui Jarvis. Used with permission.

These contextual adaptations provoked the children to make similar alterations, empathise with the characters, and produce plots that had several complex sequences of actions.

Children would regularly take characters from the storyboard to visit the Fairy Tale Café, ordering meals like, porridge with honey from the story of Goldilocks and The Three Bears or biscuits for Granny from Little Red Riding Hood (see Figure 11.5).

An excursion to a local park which dedicates itself to a range of fairy tales allowed opportunities for children to transfer their learning of fairy tale elements to many new and unfamiliar fairy tales. The children went on walks exploring different contexts, touching, feeling, smelling, and describing the spaces in detail. Older children were invited to share time with the younger children. They formed collaborative groups and responded to the contextual provocations producing written reflections and poetry.

Like little treasure hunters, magic is found everywhere; orange mushrooms on a stick might hide fairies, in holes in the trees nestle mini monsters. Hieroglyphics bored into sticks are highways for tiny bugs, long lost messages from tribes who walked this land long ago.

A long-term project, called the Mystery of Language, provides a rich understanding of spelling and words. This is explained in Box 11.2.

Box 11.2 Educators as researchers: the mystery of language
By Peter Fahey, Claire Lay, and Rebecca Ferguson

At St James Parish Primary School educators construct themselves as researchers in collaboration with the children in their class and the local community in the long-term project The Mystery of Language, which uses the story of the English language, or etymology, through multi-layered and rich investigations.

The Mystery of Language project is an example of a redesigned educational experience, moving from "the cultivation of a narrow band of skills" to providing opportunity for all, not just a few, to realise their transformational potential as active, responsible citizens of this great land. Co-participating with the children, family, community, and local place, educators recognise how the story of words and language, which traditionally begins in England, is often disconnected from the context of Australia. Specifically, in our school's case this means a disconnection with Wadawurrung Country, the local area where the school is located.

Thus, the story of language for this group begins with Wadawurrung Country and involves consultation with a local Wadawurrung woman. Central to this is a firm understanding that children, families, educators, and community are capable and contributing citizens. Collaborations with local Wadawurrung educators are a part of how teaching and learning is imagined. See Figures 11.6 to 11.9 for play scenes.

Figure 11.6 Figurines within the story of language. Photograph by Claire Lay. Used with permission.

Figure 11.7 Houses within the story of language. Photograph by Claire Lay. Used with permission.

Figure 11.8 A play scene of new people arriving. Photograph by Claire Lay. Used with permission.

This co-authored story includes detailed studies and tales of strife, invasions, struggles for power, battles for riches and farmland, and consideration of times of conflict and peace. The scenarios are a means for all children, inclusive of English-language learners, to become literate, and understand literacy as a complex process that will enable them to make meaning and communicate with audiences using the confirmed conventions of our language. Children passionately communicate their learning with genuine audiences, because they want to share their knowledge, in authentic and contextual ways. This is not an unusual project within the context of this school.

Ordinary moments as provocation

The commitment to the power of "ordinary moment" over "prescribed curriculum" is evident as staff, children and the community co-participate through The Mystery of Language project, taking on the complexity of language and literacy beyond drill and skill.

Etymology becomes a driving force, which is often regarded as being too complex for young children and more appropriate in the upper years of schooling. Educators choose to disrupt this common assumption of young

Figure 11.9 A play scene from the story of language. Photograph by Claire Lay. Used with permission.

children not being ready for this complex work, moving beyond simplistic teaching practices that view children as in deficit.

Educators regard etymology as a "story that helps connect the facts and make sense of the words in our language in meaningful ways that connect with the children's identity and purpose". This work connects with Yunkaporta's "story sharing" [Dr. Yunkaporta is a Senior Lecturer, Indigenous Knowledges, Deakin University, Geelong, Australia] where the story brings together everyone's stories and experiences, generating new knowledge through the process.

This story becomes the catalyst for this inquiry where children explore spelling through group discussion of words. For example, one child asks how to spell "knight" and this then acts as a provocation for a group discussion focused on spelling choices, histories of words, and pronunciation. Further, new words become part of their long-term memory through being connected to words, to stories and to experiences, while children continue to look for and explore dilemmas across the English language. Part of this includes asking complex questions provoked by the histories of language: Who will invade this land next?

What words will they bring? Will they be kind? Why would they invade another land?

Where did the Celts go? Will they ever know peace?

These large and complex questions illustrate the many entanglements within language and literacy. What becomes most profound for the educators, though, is that the children's wondering about words and where they come from is endless. The fear many children would have experienced (related to being able to "read and write") appears to subside. In its place is curiosity and concentration.

The Mystery of Language project situates the process of understanding and acting on literacy as social justice, with young children viewed as capable of engaging with this complexity. Spelling as part of literacy is contextual and in response to social issues where the multiple layers of language are used to understand the intentions of spelling.

Frequently asked questions

When schools are working towards embedding play-based learning, teachers and staff have many questions as they tackle the issues that arise. In this section some of these questions are presented.

How do I manage some of the really silly play that might come through, potentially from some of the older children?

Several ways of managing this could be: (1) acknowledging the child's desire to be silly in front of an audience (if this is their motivation, acknowledgement may be all they want); (2) reminding them of the importance of being respectful and responsible at school; (3) redirecting their attention to more appropriate play options and ignoring their silly behaviour; (4) providing opportunities for joke-telling at a more appropriate time. For behaviours such as this, limit setting may be required and Gary Landreth's approach of acknowledging, communicating, and targeting (ACT) can be very effective (Landreth, 2012). In essence, in this case you would

- acknowledge the feelings or motivation underlying the behaviour (e.g., you like getting attention),
- communicate the rule/limit, e.g., class time is not the place to … (describe the behaviour that is not acceptable),
- target acceptable alternatives (e.g., provide an alternative use of the objects, or propose a more challenging story in the play, or propose an action of the character that will require discussion).

How do I manage some of those big emotions and themes that present in the classroom setting that might be appropriate for therapy but not the classroom?

Some ideas have been presented in the first section of this chapter on creating a safe space. Children who cannot control their feelings and emotions need to feel safe so their emotional state can be de-escalated. A calm voice, reducing the stimulation (such as deep breathing with the child in an area away from others), and acknowledging their emotions may focus the child's attention. As teachers get to know the children in their class, they will become quicker at recognising how a child is feeling and engaging with the child to talk about their feelings, sitting with them in their uncomfortable emotions. These moments can be difficult for a teacher. A suggestion in these moments is to notice how the child feels, rather than distracting them or telling them how to feel, for example, "don't worry", or "you're okay".

An example of potentially strong emotions in the classroom is Mother's Day, which may raise emotional issues for some children. The acknowledgement of the feelings of the child and situation could take the form of: "You're feeling sad. It's Mother's Day, your mother and father have separated, and you won't see your Mum today. You can keep her card until you see her next, but it still hurts to know she's not with you today … (pause)". You can also encourage empathy and emotional understanding amongst the class by asking questions such as: "Who else has felt sad before? What does it feel like?"

Naming emotions while speaking with students in the moment, supports them to identify what the emotion feels like, and supports their ability to talk about their emotions, rather than feeling overwhelmed by them. For example, "You're feeling angry at the moment, you're really punching that play-dough hard". A teacher may extend the conservation by saying, "You punched the play-dough when you were feeling angry earlier, and now you're smiling, and your body looks more relaxed. That really worked for you. I wonder if you can tell me next time, when you are feeling frustrated or angry, and need to punch some playdough".

Children who struggle with anger often benefit from having an outlet for aggression, like punching play dough. You could also use the ACT (see prior question) to acknowledge the feelings or emotions before setting limits and targeting acceptable alternatives.

For children who frequently struggle in class, a referral for support can make a difference.

Amity Green presents the case of a child who required extra support to help him learn. By building this child's play ability, there was a reduction in the child's challenging behaviours in the classroom. John (pseudonym), was 8 years old. He had been coping at school but this particular year he would throw objects around the room and be emotionally charged whilst doing it. John's behaviour became so severe that the entire class would need to be evacuated from the classroom for fear of injuries to students and staff members. Previous teachers had not experienced this behaviour from John. A referral was made to Amity, who worked within the school. She knew that John was being taught by team teachers for the first time.

Being taught by different teachers on different days requires students to have flexibility, and to understand that one teacher's routines and behaviours in the classroom are different to another teacher's routines and behaviours in the classroom. John was very rigid in his play, and Amity worked with John to improve his flexibility in play. This shift in this play transferred to John becoming more flexible in class. He acquired the skills to cooperate and negotiate with others, and his emotional extremes lessened. Just over a month after working with John, he received an award on parade from his teachers, for significantly improved behaviour. He was observed playing for longer, both independently and with peers, and he made new friends.

In John's case, Amity had noticed that he always wanted to play with cars. He would not play anything else. The cars would drive forwards, and the cars would drive backwards. They were just cars and could be nothing but cars. In using cars to play with John, Amity began using metacommunication to describe back to John what he was doing in his play. Amity gradually added a simple storyline in her play with John. John initially just watched and continued to play in the same way that he always had done. After a couple of sessions Amity began playing "tag" with John's car, a game she had been told John enjoyed. She touched John's car, speaking in a different voice (as her car's character), and said "you're it!" John swiftly followed by tagging Amity's car with his, and a reciprocal game began, which was full of laughter. John was very excited about seeing Amity at school in the weeks following, but Amity had to work hard to shift the play each week. She began giving the cars feelings (e.g., her car might get frustrated or angry if it couldn't tag John's car easily, or she would notice John smiling and say John's car was happy). More characteristics were added for the cars, problems were introduced to the play, unstructured materials and objects were used for roads and props, which were all aimed at gradually working towards higher and higher levels of pretend play and social skill development. John began to copy and then initiate new ideas into in his own play. He extended his play to include trains and other toys that weren't vehicles. John's flexibility in play translated into flexibility in the classroom.

What does play look like for older children in Years 3–6?

Play scenes are more complex for children in Years 3–6. Complex play scenes include using small toys and unstructured objects that replicate scenes such as natural areas, cities, familiar spaces like schools and playgrounds. For this age group, play ideas extend beyond their personal experiences to include fantastic stories such as flying to another galaxy or discovering new countries. Other play suggestions are the creation of puppet plays and artistic expression (dance choreography, drama/storytelling, sculpture, painting, drawing, musical improvisation). Allow the activities to provide plenty of freedom to create, imagine, and extend ideas.

Is there any research on multi-age groupings for play?

Multi-age groupings create a zone of proximal development where children learn from each other. Christie and Stone (1999) found that in multi-age groupings (compared to same age groupings) children engaged in a larger amount and broader range of collaborative literacy activities (p. 109). They also found that play in multi-age groupings was more complex, with collaborative interactions being multi-directional (Christie & Stone, 1999). Australian Aboriginal children play in multi-age groups within their communities (Dender & Stagnitti, 2017). Mixed age groups also allow children with a range of play abilities to engage more easily, as they connect with others who are older or younger than them.

Can we set up play priority groups like we do for literacy and numeracy?

Yes, you certainly can. The information in Chapter 10 on assessment of play will help identify children who may need more experience in play and which skills in play to target in a priority group. Chapter 8 also provides examples of the "how" to embed play. Chapters 5 and 6 provide examples of whole class activities to build play ability.

Conclusion

Learning through play is very powerful when done well because it integrates the child's brain through activation of positive emotions, memory retrieval, and higher order thinking skills such as counterfactual thinking and divergent thinking. Learning through play engages the child in learning through joy, meaningful learning spaces, active "minds on" engagement, and iterative thinking, within social interaction with others (Zosh et al., 2018). This book aims to bring together research on the value of play to learning (the why), the teacher role, embedding play within the curriculum, and practical examples from several schools (the how). Embedding play for learning is a big shift in teaching pedagogy and how schools are organised, both in physical spaces and social interactions. Taking time to do it well, will provide a rich and authentic context for supporting children's cognitive, academic, physical, social, and emotional abilities, and children will be motivated to come to school. They will leave school with a strong identity as someone who can learn and contribute to their society.

References

Brandt, K., Perry, B., Seligman, S., & Tronic, E. (Eds.) (2014). *Infant and early childhood mental health: Core concepts and clinical practice*. American Psychiatric Publishing.

Brelsford, V., Meints, K., Gee, N., & Pfeffer, K. (2017). Animal-assisted interventions in the classroom: A systematic review. *International Journal of Environmental Research in Public Health*, 14, 669. doi:10.3390/ijerph14070669.

Christie, J., & Stone, S. (1999). Collaborative literacy activity in print-enriched play centers: Exploring the "zone" in same-age and multi-age groupings. *Journal of Literacy Research*, 31, 109–131 doi:10.1080/10862969909548042.

Dender, A., & Stagnitti, K. (2017). Content and cultural validity in the development of the Indigenous Play Partner Scale. *Australian Occupational Therapy Journal*, 64, 283–293. doi:10.1111/1440-1630.12355.

Jennings, S. (2017). *Creative play with children at risk*. Routledge.

Landreth, G. (2012). *Play therapy: The art of relationship* (3rd edn). Routledge.

Perry, B. D. (2013) *1: The human brain* [Video webcast]. In seven slide series. Retrieved from https://www.youtube.com/watch?v=uOsgDkeH52o.

Perry, B., Hogan, L., & Marlin, S. (2000). Curiosity, pleasure and play: A neurodevelopmental perspective. *HAAEYC Advocate*, 20, 9–12.

Siegel, D. J. (2012) *Pocket guide to interpersonal neurobiology: An integrative handbook of the mind*. W. W. Norton.

Siegel, D. J., & Bryson, T. (2012) *The whole-brain child: 12 revolutionary strategies to nurture your child's developing mind*. Bantam Books.

Stewart, A. L., Field, T. A., & Echterling, L. G. (2016). Neuroscience and the magic of play therapy. *International Journal of Play Therapy*, 25(1), 4–13. doi:10.1037/pla0000016.

Zosh, J. M., Hirsh-Pasek, K., Hopkins, E. J., Jensen, H., Liu, C., Neale, D., & Whitebread, D. (2018). Accessing the inaccessible: Redefining play as a spectrum. *Frontiers in Psychology*, 9, 1124. doi:10.3389/fpsyg.2018.01124.

Index

Page numbers in **Bold** refer to figures, page numbers in *italic* refer to tables.

For Product Safety Concerns and Information please contact our EU
representative GPSR@taylorandfrancis.com
Taylor & Francis Verlag GmbH, Kaufingerstraße 24, 80331 München, Germany

www.ingramcontent.com/pod-product-compliance
Ingram Content Group UK Ltd.
Pitfield, Milton Keynes, MK11 3LW, UK
UKHW021455080625
459435UK00012B/518